The
PURSUIT

The PURSUIT

A
Historical Biography *of*
One Family's Quest
for Life, Liberty, *and*
the Pursuit *of* Happiness
in America

JIM RUTH

Published 2024
Printed in the United States of America
Hardcover ISBN: 979-8-9909264-0-0
Paperback ISBN: 979-8-9909264-1-7
E-ISBN: 979-8-9909264-2-4
Library of Congress Control Number: 2024913336

Patriot Heritage Press
Frederick, MD
PatriotHeritagePress@gmail.com

Editing and book design by Stacey Aaronson
Cover art: Nation Makers, painted by Howard Pyle, 1906

Always grateful, never entitled.

TABLE OF CONTENTS

INTRODUCTION . . . 1

CHAPTER ONE

The Reunion . . . 5

CHAPTER TWO

The Crossing:
Braving Land and Sea . . . 15

CHAPTER THREE

Land Ho – The Delaware:
From Daydream to Reality . . . 31

CHAPTER FOUR

The Settling:
Pennsylvania Dutch Country . . . 49

CHAPTER FIVE

The Revolution:
Life, Liberty, and the Pursuit . . . 69

CHAPTER SIX

The Fledgling Republic:
A House Divided . . . 97

CHAPTER SEVEN

Westward Ho:
To the Heartland . . . 123

CHAPTER EIGHT

The World Wars:
More Sacrifices on the Altar of Freedom . . . 151

CHAPTER NINE

Arlington:
The Beautiful City of the Dead . . . 175

AFTERWORD . . . 203
ACKNOWLEDGMENTS . . . 205
NOTES . . . 209

The
PURSUIT

A Note Regarding Calendar Dates

The dates indicated in some of the diaries, letters, and manuscripts referenced in *The Pursuit* sometimes vary by about ten days due to "old style versus new style" dating. In other words, some dates were recorded using the Julian calendar while others used the Gregorian calendar.

INTRODUCTION

I had little interest in my ancestry until a chance discovery in 2020 ignited my fascination. My wife Kathy and I had purchased a second home in late March of 2006, near the beach in the small seaside town of Lewes, Delaware, at the mouth of the Delaware Bay. After I retired in 2014, we moved there from the Maryland suburbs of D.C. to live full-time. I loved going down to the ocean to walk through the surf alone with my thoughts. The smell of the salt air, the pounding waves, and the feel of wet sand between my toes was exhilarating.

Six years later, on one of those beach walks, a fleeting thought brought my attention to my first American ancestor, my fifth great-grandfather, Peter Ruth. I knew he had come to America in 1733, landing in Philadelphia. But with little interest in family genealogy and my focus on an active retirement lifestyle, I had little reason to connect the obvious ancestral dots. That is, until I stood staring across the water into the mouth of the Delaware Bay. In that moment, I realized that Peter Ruth and his family must have sailed right past Lewes on their way to Philadelphia.

Unlike me, my wife Kathy was intrigued by family genealogy and had used Ancestry.com for many years. When I returned home that day, I started digging around in her account. Kathy's seed work made my initial plunge into my family tree easy, and I soon found myself

Googling everything from passenger manifests and graveyard listings to land surveys and census records. Each query led me to more enticing pieces of my family's historical puzzle.

Before long, I was hooked. One of my early discoveries was a diary written by one of the passengers on Peter's ship. Another gem I unearthed was a letter describing their harrowing passage across the Atlantic written by another voyager to his son back in Switzerland. Both accounts confirmed that Peter's ship, the *Pennsylvania Merchant*, not only sailed past Lewes but dropped anchor there for the night only hundreds of yards off the beach I had just walked on. In fact, Lewes was the first land Peter saw in America. That discovery unlocked a flood of revelations about his journey to America, his family's settling in the Pennsylvania Dutch country, and his fourteen children and their descendants.

Despite persistent Indian attacks, the French and Indian War, and the Revolution, the Ruths prospered farming the land with their children. Their grit and determination spawned a family tree with branches extending deep and wide into American life and history. The eight sons of Peter and Sophia—and later Catharine, Peter's wife after Sophia died— fought in America's war for independence, while other patriots in the Ruth family tree made enduring contributions to our fledgling country. They answered the Lexington Alarm, the first armed skirmishes of the Revolution; they fought against British General Burgoyne in the battles at Saratoga and clashed with traitor Benedict Arnold in the Battle of New London. And on a British prison ship in New York City's harbor, one drew his last breath.

Nearly ninety years later, they fought in some of the bloodiest battles of the Civil War to save the Union and purge the United States of slavery. Nine volunteered for service in the Union Army: five were killed in action by the Rebels or died later of battle wounds or from sickness or disease. Among the survivors, only three returned home, seemingly unscathed, and one suffered a lifelong paralyzing injury.

In the years that followed, an ancestor who volunteered for the Indiana Infantry served in the Spanish-American War. Another, a twenty-six-year-old Marine corporal, was wounded by mustard gas during World War I while fighting in the trenches of France against advancing enemy soldiers. His cousin, a young lawyer from Chicago, was killed in action charging a German machine-gun nest. In feeder branches of the family tree, during World War II, a young navigator's B-24 was shot out of the sky on a bombing mission over Nazi-occupied Europe; he evaded capture for nearly five months with the help of Belgian resistance fighters. Another landed on Utah Beach on D-Day plus one, only to die in France nearly six weeks later in the Battle for Normandy.

The roots and branches of my family legacy extend well beyond America's battlefields, however. The vast majority were not heroic soldiers, but rather average Joes and Janes—people who worked hard every day to provide for their families. They helped to settle America's heartland, pushing its boundaries farther west toward the Pacific, quietly building the United States of America into the great nation it is today.

Initially, I set out to write a short history of my forebears, but in the process, I discovered it was not my family's story alone. Yes, it is a quintessentially American tale, but it is also the story of America itself. With this revelation, my research grew into something much more expansive than I imagined, and that is the book you now hold in your hands.

The Pursuit tells the story through the eyes of my ancestors and their contemporaries. Each chapter is immersed in historical background, giving context to the world they encountered and the turbulent times in which they lived. It reveals how they traversed great distances and overcame daunting obstacles. I uncovered these details by spending countless hours examining diaries, letters, passenger manifests, provincial council proceedings, and state militia and war department records. I also consulted church and historical society journals, American history books, and family genealogical records. Some of the language quoted in these documents doesn't neatly conform to modern writing styles, but when patched together, the excerpts taken from those accounts—even with their spelling and grammatical blunders—bring an authenticity that breathes life into otherwise tedious historical facts.

Through the wars they fought, the sorrows they suffered, the joys they celebrated, and the aspirations they pursued, my ancestors' stories read like a patchwork quilt of sacrifice, courage, and achievement, each in pursuit of their own American dream.

Perhaps you will see your own American dream in theirs.

CHAPTER ONE

The Reunion

*L*ong before I took a deep dive into my family's ancestry, on a late Friday afternoon in mid-September of 1983, my wife, kids, and I pulled into the parking lot of the Abraham Lincoln Motor Inn in Reading, Pennsylvania. We were in town for a historic gathering of the Ruth clan in Sinking Spring, just down the road. The reunion organizer, a distant cousin, recommended the inn as one of several for the weekend event. With a young family in tow and a tight budget, I checked the list for the cheapest lodging accommodation available and booked the reservation.

After registering at the front desk, Kathy and I, trailed by our daughter Heather and son Michael, stepped into the antiquated elevator—our first inkling that something might be amiss. After groaning up several flights, the old lift finally reached our floor. We made our way down the dimly lit hallway and found our room. As we walked through the door, we were assaulted by stained walls, peeling lead paint on the windows, and beds covered with tattered spreads. The look on Kathy's face told me we would not be spending the night at Mr. Lincoln's Motor Inn.

Downstairs, the desk clerk in the lobby was very understanding as I anxiously fabricated a tale about an emergency back home in Maryland requiring our immediate departure. We loaded ourselves and our luggage back into the car and headed down the road, grateful to find a vacancy at the Sheraton Berkshire Inn before the reunion commenced the following afternoon. Though the rooms cost more than I had planned to spend, I would soon find out it was worth splurging for a weekend our family would never forget.

The gathering had been planned for Saturday, September 18th, to commemorate the fateful date Peter Ruth landed in Philadelphia 250 years earlier. With a buzz of anticipation in the air, at 1:00 p.m. a caravan of nearly thirty cars brimming with cousins—from as far away as California and Florida, and representing fifteen states—lined up like a funeral procession. White banners with *Ruth* printed on them waved from every window, eager for the grand tour.[1] Within minutes, our intrepid guide, Dr. James A. Ruth of Wyomissing, led the way to three historic Ruth-family properties, making quick stops or slow drive-bys at each location. Each one held its own fascination, but these were only a warmup.

From here, heading west out of Sinking Spring, we turned off Route 422 onto an unmarked, one-lane country road. Traveling several hundred yards to the crest of a gently sloping hill, then down into a picturesque little valley, we were greeted by a large stone house and two-story Pennsylvania Dutch barn, just across a branch of the Cacoosing Creek. The rolling country lane, it turned out, was the driveway leading to one of Peter Ruth's original homes.

Lucky for us, the current owner, Mrs. Herman Miller, allowed members of the Ruth expedition to roam the property for about an hour. Though we were not granted permission to enter the house or barn, we were able to admire the original stone structure Peter built, with chimneys at each end. Tasteful additions on both sides of the home had increased its size considerably, but the fruits of Peter's labor were still intact and well preserved. As Tom Gerhart, president of the Pennsylvania German Society, told me in June of 2021, "When they build a stone house, they don't move."

The Ruth Mansion. Photo by Jim Ruth, 1983.

From the reunion handout, we learned that the "Ruth Mansion" was built on a tract of about 431 acres, land Peter purchased from Thomas Bartholomew and his wife Catherine on January 16, 1748, nearly fifteen years after Peter landed in America. The "consideration" exchanged for the purchase of the land was "the Sum of Six Hundred Pounds lawful money of Pennsylvania"[2]—the "lawful money" of the day being the British Pound Sterling. Today, 600 pounds equals nearly $161,000 in US dollars after adjusting for inflation. When Peter died twenty-three years later, he had amassed total land holdings of almost double: "857 acres, 21 perches," to be exact.[3] (A perch is an old English unit of measurement equaling sixteen and a half feet, taking the total to 857.131 acres.)

We further learned, taken from the 1916 History of the *St. John's (Hain's) Reformed Church*:

> The present Henry Gaul farm—a Ruth homestead—deserves special attention. It lies in a broad sweep of the valley more than a quarter of a mile from the public highway. The main part of the house dates back to about the time of the Revolution. . . . Double floors, with the space between the timbers filled solid with mortar, are a feature in the construction of the house. A beautiful meadow stream—a branch of the Cacoosing—and a group of three grand buttonwood trees overtopping the farm buildings by more than fifty feet.[4]

With visions of Peter's magnificent home still in my head, we made the short drive to St. John's Reformed Church, on Penn Avenue/Route 422. The location was noteworthy because in 1793, the land for the church and cemetery was donated by Christian, Peter's son. He had inherited the land from his father and bequeathed it to the church in his will, saying, "I give and devise one acre and a half of land as will be most suitable for the use of a new Reformed Church and burial ground . . . to the congregation and their heirs and successors forever."[5] He and four of his brothers (Peter, George, John, and Henry) are buried there along with numerous other descendants of the Ruth family. Though many of the eighteenth-century stones that remained had deteriorated significantly and were mostly unintelligible after nearly three hundred years of wind, water, and weather, it was still awe-inspiring to see their final resting places.

After leaving the church, our reunion caravan drove by several other Ruth properties before turning onto Columbia Avenue/Fritztown Road. Several miles away was the first homestead of Peter and Sophia Ruth. The log house and barn he and his young sons built were no longer there, of course, but their stone-spring house, the family's source of fresh water and food storage, was still standing. We wandered around the old farmstead for a while, taking in the sights, trying to imagine what it was like for Peter and his family as pioneers in virgin territory all those years ago. After that, we piled back into our cars and headed for Denver, a tiny Pennsylvania town about ten miles west.

Tucked away in the middle of a cornfield, an old family burial plot awaited us. The day before, the accommodating farmer who owned the property used his combine machine to cut a wide swath through the corn rows so our line of cars could enter and circle the gravesite—a three-and-a-half-foot-high masonry wall that guarded the rectangular family burial ground. As with the church cemetery, most of the gravestones were severely weatherworn and illegible after centuries of exposure to the elements. The remains of many of Peter's grandchildren, their spouses, and his great-grandchildren were interred here, and we were able to pay our respects. Afterward, the Ruth convoy headed back toward Sinking Spring, dispersing along the way to our respective hotels.

Later that evening, we met up again at the Blue Velvet restaurant in Robesonia, a small town nearby. Following a cocktail hour and buffet-style dinner, several speakers entertained us with interesting ancestral stories and anecdotes from the past. This was when I learned that among our ancestors, we have at least one United States Senator, Charles Percy of Illinois; several congressmen; and a slew of state legislators. But what piqued my interest the most were the whispers about a Nobel Peace Prize winner in our family tree. Later, my research revealed that Jane Addams, born in 1860 and one of the world's most influential social reformers of her day, shared lineage from my fifth great-grandmother, Catharine Meyer, Peter's second wife. As far as I could determine, she was also the first feminist in our extended family.

Jane was indeed a Prize recipient, sharing the honor in 1931 with another American "for their assiduous effort to revive the ideal of peace and to rekindle the spirit of peace in their own nation and in the whole of mankind," according to the Nobel citation. Sadly, her poor health that December prevented her from attending the ceremony in Oslo, Norway.

Only four years later, in 1935, Jane died at the age of 74. The funeral was held in the courtyard of her beloved Hull House in Chicago, where she ministered to the city's impoverished immigrant community. Modeled after settlement houses in England, Hull House offered educational programs, healthcare, childcare, and employment services. Addams also fought for child labor laws and helped immigrants become US citizens. Her worldwide acclaim as a social reformer grew through her writings and speeches promoting social reform and peace. She was a vocal opponent of World War I, often publicly chastising President Woodrow Wilson because she believed all wars sapped a country's ability to help its most disadvantaged citizens.

I further uncovered that Jane's father, John H. Addams, was a native of Sinking Spring who worked as a banker, agricultural businessman, and Illinois state senator. He was also a Civil War veteran and personal friend of Abraham Lincoln. Letters from the president addressed to her father always opened with the salutation, "My Dear Double D-'ed Addams." Jane reportedly adored her father, and it's probably safe to assume that her fiery activism for social issues, both at home and abroad, was influenced by his civic involvement. Growing up in the shadow of slavery in a privileged, politically active family, she had a front-row seat to America's melting pot, witnessing firsthand the divide between the "haves" and the "have-nots." She could probably never have imagined how profoundly her activism would inspire future generations of women. "What after all has maintained the human race on this old globe despite all the calamities of nature and all the tragic failings of mankind," said Addams, "if not faith in new possibilities and courage to advocate [for] them." Quite a pleasant surprise to find her in my ancestral line.

On the final day of the reunion, Kathy and I, along with our kids, my parents, and my brother and his family, returned to nearby Wernersville and the St. John's (Hain's) Reformed Church. We wanted one last opportunity to explore the grounds, particularly the old cemetery.

Perched near the top of a hill, the church and the old burial ground overlooked the valley below. Tacked to the western wall of the historic brick structure was a weathered bronze plaque. Tarnished over a span of more than five decades, it paid homage to fifty parishioners who fought for independence in the Revolution. Among the names listed were three of Peter's sons and his grandson: Sergeant Adam Ruth, Jacob and Michael Ruth, and Michael's son Christian Ruth. We all stood silently reflecting on how those emblazoned on that memorial tablet, along with countless other patriots throughout the colonies, risked everything they had for the cause of life, liberty, and the pursuit of happiness in America.

The historic plaque was erected by the Commonwealth of Pennsylvania in tandem with the Berks County Chapter of the Daughters of the American Revolution in 1931. These men, who signed oaths of allegiance to the cause and would have been seen as traitors to their former English masters, risked everything to take up arms for independence. "These brave souls took to the field of battle against the world's greatest superpower of the age, the British Empire, in order that they and future millions would be free from tyranny. For this we can all be thankful and proud."[6]

Before we left the cemetery grounds, we roamed the aging stones once more. While trying to decipher the names on the weather-worn markers, we stumbled upon one we could just barely make out: the gravestone of Peter's eldest child, Michael. It had been dutifully marked with a small American flag and a tarnished DAR medallion.

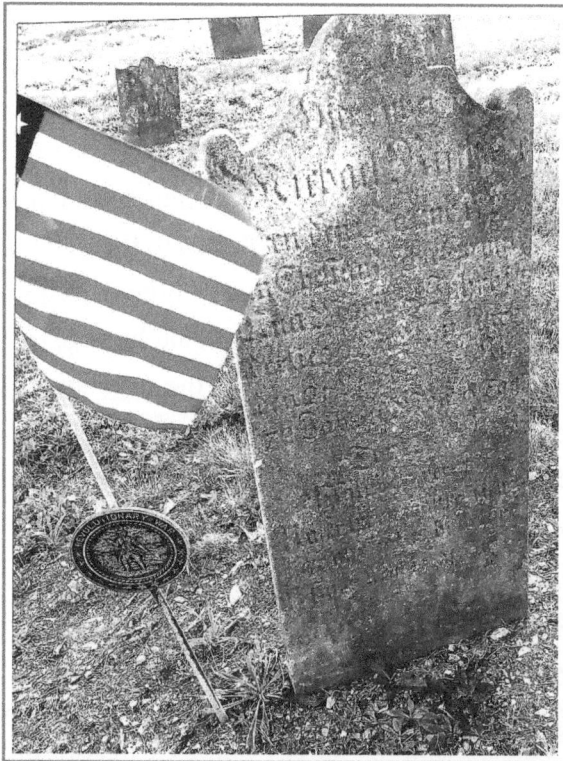

Michael Ruth's grave at St. John's (Hain's) Reformed Church in Wernersville, PA.
Photo by Jim Ruth, June 2021.

Years later, in early June of 2021, I took a road trip to Sinking Spring from my home (at that time) in Lewes, Delaware, and made a surprising and disappointing discovery: In the 1950s and early '60s, many of the earliest grave markers along Penn Avenue were removed. They were "neglected and dangerous," said the *200th Anniversary Edition, Saint John's United Church of Christ*, a church history published in 1992.[7] The historic grave markers were replaced with open, green space now marked with several memorial stones honoring the service of veterans of various American wars, including the Revolution.

A Peter Ruth descendant told me that the decision to remove the old gravestones was highly contentious among church members, and the measure only passed by one vote. The gravestones removed were reportedly offered to local descendants of the deceased parishioners, while unclaimed stones were disrespectfully "tossed in the woods," according to a groundskeeper I spoke with that day.

Among the gravestones apparently discarded were those of Christian and his wife, Barbara. The Wernersville St. John's (Hain's) Church's historical records mention the burial ground at the St. John's Reformed Church in Sinking Spring, stating, "Christian Ruth's grave and that of his wife can be found side by side to the west of the church building."[8] Today, immediately to the west of the church building is the site of the green space.

The local Ruth family descendants I spoke with have no recollection of ever being contacted regarding the disposition of those historic gravestones. Christian's "forever" gift to the congregation and their heirs rang hollow to future generations of churchgoers—a tragic end for the proud American patriot who donated the land on which the church's parishioners have worshiped for nearly 230 years.

When we finally headed home from the reunion, with Sinking Spring in the rearview mirror, I replayed the places we had been privileged to visit and the fascinating ancestral history we had learned. But it was the long shadow cast by Peter's beautiful, old stone home that particularly held my interest. Though I wouldn't return for nearly twenty-five years, that house, along with the memories of that 1983 reunion weekend, would keep a spark of my family's remarkable American journey alive.

1983 Family Reunion Weekend
Top row: (L-R) Jim Ruth, the author; Robert, Jim's father; Bob, Jim's brother;
Heather, Jim's daughter. Middle row: Michael, Jim's son; John and Cindy, Bob's
kids. Bottom row: Diane, Bob's daughter; Kathy, Bob's wife, with their dog
Whiskey; Virginia, mother of Jim and Bob; Kathy, Jim's wife.

CHAPTER TWO

The Crossing:
Braving Land and Sea

*O*n the other side of the Atlantic Ocean, in a tiny village called Walhausen in a country then known as Prussia, Johann Peter Ruth imagined a new beginning for his family on the North American continent. He was no doubt aware of the dangerous and unforgiving odds of successfully navigating great distances by land and sea to a virgin territory with his family in tow, but that didn't stop him from dreaming.

Johann Peter (who was called Peter) was born to Melchior and Catharina Ruth in the tiny village of Steinberg around 1700. The exact date of his birth is uncertain, and little is known about his early life in Germany. But what we do know is that in the old country, Peter's family were landowners who worked as farmers and artisans—stonecutters and masons, master tailors and tanners, blacksmiths, and cartwrights.

Sometime in his midtwenties, Peter met Anna Sophia Lauer, who, like Peter, went by her middle name. On February 15, 1724, in the tiny village of Wolfersweiler, Peter married his nearly twenty-one-year-old bride and the newlyweds settled in Walhausen in southwestern Germany, east of the Moselle River, about two and a half miles west of where they were married.

The previous hundred-plus years in Peter's homeland had been brutal. The Thirty Years War (1618–1648), one of the most destructive in European history, had left as many as eight million civilians and soldiers dead. In some parts of Germany, 60 percent of the entire civilian population was lost. Forty years later, Germany struggled through another devastating conflict: the Nine Years War (1688–1697), a bloodbath that was dubbed the War of the Palatinate by Rhinelanders. French soldiers, under orders from King Louis XIV, burned, looted, and pillaged Peter's homeland. For nearly a year, the army of the Sun King "implemented a large-scale, systematic scorched-earth policy from Cologne to Freiburg."[1]

Included in the devastation were villages, churches, castles, and entire cities, such as Heidelberg and Mannheim. The French aimed to render Germany completely helpless—destroying its means and fortifications—so it would be unable to wage resistance at home or invade France in the future. All of this death and destruction happened a few years before Peter's birth, but the memories were all too real for his parents.

The remnants of the old Holy Roman Empire left in its wake a fragmented collection of independent states that were only unified when Frederick of Brandenburg (Frederick William I) was crowned King of Prussia in 1713. He soon engaged Prussia in the Great Northern War. When this war ended in 1721, the King of Prussia's nation-state had gained precious seaports along the Baltic Sea coast. His successful alliance with Russia's Peter the Great ended the Swedish Empire's tight grip on access to Baltic harbors. Although his army was used sparingly during his twenty-seven-year reign, Frederick William I, known as the Soldier King, built the most formidable fighting force in all of Europe.

I can imagine that the accumulation of these traumatic events weighed heavily on Peter Ruth's mind, and he was almost certainly burdened with questions: Would he be drafted into the Prussian army for a future war? Would the continued fighting lead to the devastation, famines, and plagues that his parents' generation had experienced? And then there were the glowing accounts of German settlers prospering in Pennsylvania without religious or political persecution. Were those stories true? Was that kind of life possible? Was he enticed by the promise of cheap land in William Penn's colony?

Any or all of these factors could have convinced Peter to trade the harsh certainty of eighteenth-century Prussian life for a chance to pursue the promise of his daydreams, leaving behind the land of his birth. But what we do know for certain is this: Peter was a farmer who worked the land with his bare hands. The lure of inexpensive land all his own—rich, charcoal-brown soil he could pinch between his fingers—must have been intoxicating.

Peter couldn't have known the landscape that awaited him in America—its interior inhabited mainly by Native Americans, except for a handful of bustling cities that hugged its eastern coast. Those cities were largely populated by European settlers, and most were English. But there was an enclave in the middle Atlantic region, just west of Philadelphia, that was mainly populated by Germans from the tormented middle Rhine region where Peter lived. Word traveled about this new German-inhabited hamlet far to the west in North America, and it was to that place that Peter's dreams took him.

After over nine years of tending his land as a farmer, and with four sons now ranging in age from almost nine (Michael) to almost two (Peter), with twins Jacob and Christian nearly seven,[2] Peter made the monumental decision in late spring 1733 to set sail with his young family for America.

This decision may have been filled with hope but was nonetheless fraught with enormous risk and sacrifice. The daunting journey ahead would involve crossings of both land and sea, demanding tremendous fortitude and dogged determination from the entire family.

Determining what to pack and what to leave behind was likely difficult for both Peter and Sophia. With a horse- or ox-drawn cart to transport their belongings—or possibly only a handcart—they would have been forced to stow only the essential gear required in the new country or needed aboard the ship during their voyage. In addition to food, they likely packed a small iron stove and kettle, as well as farming and woodworking tools: an ax for felling trees, a grubbing hoe for digging dirt, an auger for drilling holes, and rasps for shaping rough-hewn wood. The last of the essentials would have included the family Bible, which recorded important dates—their wedding day and their children's birth and baptismal dates. And then, only if space permitted, a few sentimental items would be tucked away as reminders of the family and the life they would forever leave behind.

The Ruths' extended journey would commence with an overland trek, probably to Trier, a bustling city of five thousand-plus inhabitants, perched beside the Moselle River. As the crow flies, it was only about thirty-five miles from their home in Walhausen. But it would have been a much longer distance following the meandering earthen roads of the time, requiring three or more days of travel.

After reaching Trier, the Ruths probably chartered a small boat to sail them downriver past Cochem to Koblenz on the Rhine River. The mighty Rhine flows north to the sea, propelled by massive snow melts in the Swiss Alps to the south. There, they likely boarded a larger vessel to continue their passage down the Rhine, north past Bonn and

Cologne, all the way to the seaport city of Rotterdam, more than 300 river miles north in the Netherlands.

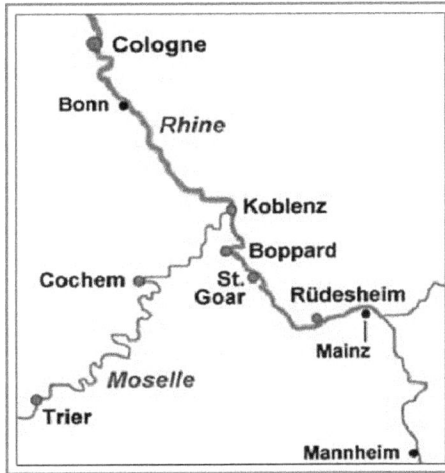

Trier on the Moselle River is shown on the lower left. Koblenz is in the center with the Rhine River running diagonally lower right to upper left past Cologne toward Rotterdam in the Netherlands. Map courtesy of European Castles Tour.

Reckoning from sixteen-year-old voyager David Scholtze's diary—where he describes his voyage up the Elbe River to Amsterdam[3]—the Ruths' voyage to the Netherlands would have probably taken three to five weeks. (Scholtze later became Peter's shipmate on their voyage to America.) Based on Scholtze's account of river travel—assuming the Ruths had a similar experience—their passage on the Rhine likely averaged five to ten miles a day. Each leg down the river presented numerous obstacles to impede their progress: shifting tides and unfavorable winds, ever-changing currents, elusive sandbars, and floating debris—all in addition to other barges and boat traffic on the busy Rhine waterway.

The Ruths must have made multiple stops along their passage, including mandatory pauses at customs houses to pay taxes and tolls for the right to travel the great river. They would also dock their vessel for overnight layovers and to restock provisions for their journey. In those days, streams and rivers were the main thoroughfares for passenger and commercial traffic. Today, by car, the same journey from Walhausen to Rotterdam, traveling on state roads and the autobahn, would be an easy five-hour drive—and that's assuming several pit stops for gas, food, and potty breaks along the way.

As the Ruths sailed into Rotterdam, they must have been filled with excitement and anticipation as their eyes scanned the bustling harbor brimming with sailing ships bound for destinations near and far. Once their boat was secured at the dock, they would have gathered their belongings, leaving their river transport for the last time. From there, they probably headed along the waterfront in search of a particular vessel—a brigantine with two main masts, square-rigged with triangular rigging both fore and aft—bound for England.

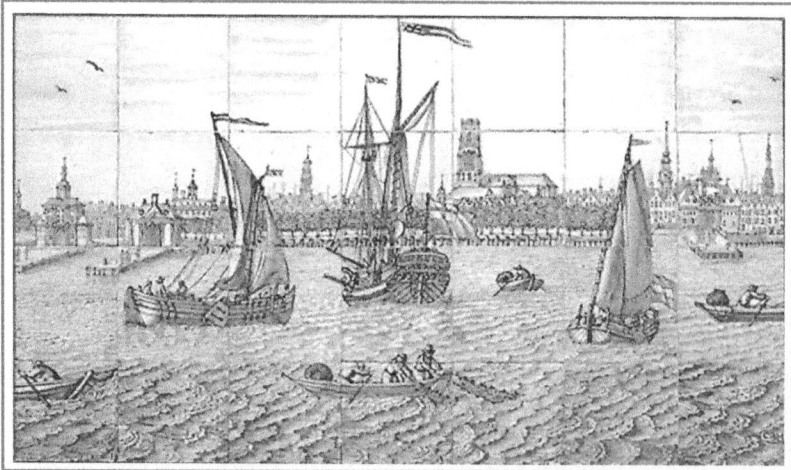

View of Rotterdam between 1700 and 1720.
Painted on tile by Dutch artist Cornelis Boumeester.

The waterfront was undoubtedly swarming with hardy stevedores and roustabouts, loading and off-loading cargo. Peter likely hired one of these rugged dockworkers to haul his possessions to the sailing ship that would carry him and his family to America. I imagine them elbowing their way through the teeming wharf to find their ship and its captain, then after settling the fare for passage, trudging up the boarding plank to the ship's main deck with all their worldly belongings in hand. From there, they would have disappeared below deck to stake a claim on the tiny, six-by-six-foot space that would be their home for the next three months.

Some days later, on June 24, 1733, the Ruths set sail from Rotterdam in their brigantine, the *Pennsylvania Merchant*, with Mr. John Steadman as their captain.[4] "Our ship carried only 155 tons," wrote Scholtze on the 28th, "but there were over 300 persons on board so that we were much crowded."

During this period, ships typically carried between 150 and 300 (or more) passengers to American ports. Historical records show that, between 1730 and 1734, the average number of German immigrants on each ship was 189 souls, not including crew.[5] If there were over 300 passengers onboard the *Pennsylvania Merchant* in Rotterdam, as David Scholtze states in his diary, more than 100 people must have disembarked in England before the voyage to America. Provincial Council records in Philadelphia show that only 187 persons "were imported here in the brigantine *Pennsylvania Merchant*, [with Captain] John Stedman."[6]

The journey to England did not start well. On the first afternoon, the ship ran aground on a sand bar, causing a delay of several hours. Bad luck dogged them the next day, too, as good sailing wind seemed to evaporate. Nevertheless, they pressed on, navigating the inland shoals and waterways of Rotterdam, with layovers of one to three days at several ports along the way.

Finally, on the afternoon of July 5, 1733, the *Merchant* reached the sea. Scholtze noted that in a short time, everyone became seasick, but that the wind was fair, and they had sight of Flanders and the Spanish Netherlands. Toward evening, they saw Calais on the French coast, and the next day, the chalk cliffs of Dover in England.[7]

After six days on choppy seas, in the early morning of July 11, tragedy struck. The first of many deaths onboard came with the passing of a child who had been ill since leaving Rotterdam. "Its body was enclosed in a sack with some sand," wrote Scholtze, "and after singing the hymn, 'Nun lasset uns den Leib begraben,'[8] was sunk by the sailors into the ocean. Such is the manner of burial at sea."[9]

With heavy hearts, no doubt, they pressed on after the loss and the ship arrived happily at Plymouth, England, two days later . . . "[where] our Captain took in fresh water and provisions and settled the toll."[10]

After spending nineteen days at sea out of Rotterdam, the voyagers probably hoped their ship would tie up at the dock, offering one last opportunity to disembark and feel solid ground under their feet—but this was not to be. Instead, during the eight-day layover, they "had to lie in the middle of the harbor until the ship was cleared by customs and provisioned."[11]

As the sun was setting on the 21st of July, the captain was finally able to set a course to follow the stars to North America. By the next evening, the Palatine voyagers saw the last of the coast of England,[12] and over the next eleven days at sea, they sailed past eight ships bound for the continent of Europe. Most were merchant ships returning from the West Indies with cargo holds brimming with barrels of rum, molasses, and sugar. Scholtze wrote on July 28th: "Early in the morning about 3 o'clock, [we] met a French Man-of-War. . . . It sailed around our ship and made many inquiries of our Captain. Its name was 'La Elizabeth.' They used speaking-trumpets" to talk to each other.[13]

As exciting as this leg of the journey may have felt, the hardships of crossing the brutal Atlantic Ocean were just beginning. Not only would the pilgrims have to endure the hazards of wind, weather, and currents, but there would be other troubling concerns awaiting them: sickness, sweltering heat, scurvy, and rats, to name a few. But another common enemy also assaulted passengers and crew alike: the disagreeable food. Compared to the traditional meals they ate in their homeland—wheaten bread and biscuits, butter, roasts, cheese, fruits, vegetables, and plentiful quantities of beer and wine—the sustenance of life shipboard, by all accounts, was awful. Noted Klaus Wust in an article about the dismal state of culinary fare aboard Palatine vessels: "A ship's fare consisted mainly of items that would keep reasonably well for months such as hardtack, flour, peas, beans, rice, preserved meats, and aged cheese . . . and its heavy salt content made even strong individuals susceptible to a variety of illnesses."[14]

Before leaving port, fresh fruits, vegetables, and other provisions were always loaded onboard whenever available, but their limited shelf life meant the short supply was usually depleted in a few weeks. Wust adds: "Moreover, seasickness, especially during the first days of the voyage, prevented many passengers from eating regularly while supplies were still fresh." Adding to their predicament was that "after two or three weeks at sea, water turned increasingly putrid, beer became sour, and grain products [turned] humid and alive with vermin."[15] To replace tainted water, the passengers had to capture runoff rainwater from the sails—with luck, they could sometimes gather as much as thirty gallons in a heavy downpour.

Voyagers had been forewarned to bring additional food with them, and those who heeded that advice packed aged cheese, dried fruit and meat, and hefty quantities of beer, wine, bread, butter, and biscuits, according to Wust. However, John Naas, in a letter written to his son back in Switzerland, describes that many who brought foodstuffs onboard with them foolishly tapped into their provisions almost immediately, passing up the ship's fare while it was still relatively palatable. This was a miscalculation they would sorely regret.[16]

One of the few bright spots, however, in the bleak shipboard culinary fare was when the crew could hook or harpoon large fish—shark, tuna, dolphin, and the like. According to Naas's letter, one such incident occurred on September 7th when one of the sailors caught a shark. They used a large iron hook as "thick as a finger" and "bated it with one and a half pounds of bacon." Sailors hauled their catch over the rail onto the deck "with such force that if it had hit someone's legs, they would certainly have been crushed." Captain Steadman took great pleasure in dispensing chunks of fresh fish to the voyagers, hacked into portions by the ship's carpenter.[17]

As one might imagine, after being confined below deck in dark, damp, and crowded quarters, the typically amiable voyagers started to show the strain of weeks at sea. With deplorable food, putrid water, and frightful storms thrown into the mix—not to mention a grim death toll as a dozen fellow travelers would perish before they dropped anchor in Philadelphia—passengers naturally grew edgy.

Reflected Naas: "It makes my heart sorrowful to recall that often aboard ship," there was "swearing, blasphemy, nagging, and fighting, swilling and gorging and quarreling day and night. . . . Neighbors accused one another . . . instead of helping one another. Living so close together on a ship for thirteen or fourteen or fifteen weeks where they cannot do as they please brings out the worst in them."[18]

With little to amuse or entertain the pilgrims on their long voyage, it's not surprising that the relentless monotony of rolling seas, recurring squalls, and the tedium of their daily routine made them irritable and weary. When available, beer and wine provided an occasional respite from fear, their relentless shipboard companion. Another welcome distraction was an occasional fist-fighting match. Scholtze says in his account, "The Captain and the boatswain had a boxing match in which the Captain came off best." The boatswain, the shipboard equivalent of a construction foreman, directed the work activities of the other seamen. Undoubtedly, the "bos'n" was aware of shipboard politics and mindful that besting his boss in front of his sailors and the passengers would probably not lead to a good outcome. The other distractions were more sobering, as burials at sea occurred more often than anyone anticipated. Over the course of their voyage to America, the Naas and Scholtze accounts reveal at least nine young children or babies perished, along with three women. All were victims of sickness, accident, or birthing on a merciless voyage across perilous waters.

Despite all of these harsh realities, however, the voyagers were lucky to have John Steadman as their captain—a man who would develop a sterling reputation among German emigrants on this and future crossings. Many commanders didn't honor their contracts and shortchanged their passengers on promised food, water, and other essential foodstuffs; passenger accounts are rife with stories of foul treatment by cruel and vindictive masters. But Steadman was not one of them. Not only was he "a very good captain," according to Christopher Schultze, who sailed on the *Saint Andrew* into Philadelphia one year after the Ruth family arrived, but he "kept strictly to his contract, [with] very able sailors, who had very much patience with us."[19]

Steadman's reputation reached far beyond being a trustworthy and humane captain. Navigating the oceans in the eighteenth century was both art and science, and miscalculations of either could be deadly. The art part of the equation involved the seafaring experience of a salty, veteran sea captain; the science piece required the certainty of the stars and the skillful use of two mechanical instruments.

For mariners, there are two kinds of stars in the sky: those that rise and set, and those that are fixed in the same place night after night, like Polaris, often called the North Star. Stars that rise and set always follow the same path through the heavens from east to west, beginning and ending their journey below the horizon. A sailor could successfully traverse the ocean over thousands of miles with remarkable accuracy by locating these stars and using a navigational device.

Captain Steadman, a seasoned mariner with two previous Atlantic crossings, probably navigated using a Davis quadrant, rather than a sextant. The sextant had been invented only two years earlier in 1731 and proved expensive, bulky, and unwieldy to manipulate. In contrast, the quadrant, introduced in 1595 by Captain John Davis while searching for the Northwest Passage, was a tried-and-true device that remained in use for over 150 years.

As Steadman's ship was sailing in waters above the equator, his primary mission was to spot Polaris. Having accomplished that, he could "line the sights of the quadrant up with Polaris . . . located directly over the North Pole," says a publication of the Ponce de Leon Inlet Lighthouse & Museum. "Because of its location, Polaris never sets like the other stars in the night sky." By "lining the star up in the quadrant's sights," the captain "could determine their latitude by measuring the angle (or elevation) between the horizon and Polaris."[20] Latitude determines the distance of a point on the north-south axis from the equator; longitude identifies the distance of a point on the east-west axis from the Prime Meridian.

The other navigational instrument used by Captain Steadman to guide the *Pennsylvania Merchant* was a compass. Commonly used by Eastern European sailors since the early eleventh century, a compass indicates the direction—north, south, east, or west—the wind is pushing a vessel. Under the watchful eye of voyager John Naas during the whole trip, Steadman was on the top deck checking it regularly to see if a change of course took place.[21]

As with any seafaring venture, the most foreseeable of all possible adversities was the unpredictability of the weather—and it rarely disappointed. The weather could be a mariner's best friend or his mortal enemy. With calm seas and plentiful wind pushing their sails, it could mean a smooth and quick passage. "But even with the best wind the voyage lasts seven weeks," wrote Gottlieb Mittelberger on a later voyage to America. And, "unless they have good wind, [they] must often sail eight, nine, ten to twelve weeks before they reach Philadelphia."[22]

In mid-August, violent storms continued stalking the *Pennsylvania Merchant*, some lasting two full days or more. John Naas confided to his son: "All of the sails had to be lashed, the rudder tied, and the portholes covered with boards. We sat in darkness while the force of the waves broke through the glass into the beds . . . and the ship was left at the mercy of the wind and waves." Many of the passengers were "running and vomiting."[23] In the vernacular of the day, "running" meant diarrhea.

With evening approaching on September 19th and winds blowing southwest, David Scholtze made an ominous entry in his diary:

A violent storm arose during the night. It wrenched off the bolt from one of the port hole-shutters and a terrible quantity of water poured into the ship. In the morning the waves were fearful, like rocky cliffs and high mountains. The noise of their roaring was horrible. It was a spectacle awful to witness.[24]

A captain is sometimes required to make life-or-death decisions for the survival of the ship and its passengers. In Gottlieb Mittelberger's 1750 voyage, the captain was left to make a heartbreaking decision: "One day, just as we had a heavy gale," reveals Mittelberger, "a woman in our ship, who was to give birth and could not under the circumstances of the storm, was pushed through the porthole and dropped into the sea. . . . Because she was far in the rear of the ship . . . [it] could not be brought forward [to rescue her]."

Eighteenth-century two-masted brigantine—square-rigged with triangular rigging fore and aft—in choppy seas, by Brigitte Werner via Pixabay.

On the *Merchant,* the next day brought no respite from violent weather as another storm brutalized their tiny vessel. "The water came into the ship with such force that many people's bedrolls which lay by portholes were completely wet," Naas wrote. "In great haste, all holes were quickly closed, the rudder bound, and the ship set sideways against the wind with close rigged sails so that it did not roll so much to both sides."[25] During violent storms, no one would remain topside on the main deck except a sailor tied to the rudder who held watch. Everyone else, says Naas, including the captain and the steersman, remained below deck to wait out the storm, soaked to the bone in their sopping clothes, anticipating the long-awaited site of land.

CHAPTER THREE

Land Ho – The Delaware: From Daydream to Reality

teadman could feel it in his bones. Sensing that land was near, he started taking depth soundings. "At midnight the first sounding was taken," wrote John Naas, "over one hundred fifty fathoms deep without finding bottom."[1]

The next morning, the captain's search continued. At nine o'clock, he finally found the bottom at fifty-five fathoms, a depth of 330 feet. Two hours later, the bottom was at thirty-five fathoms, then twenty. But there was still no land in sight.

Two days later, in the early morning of September 24, 1733, after surviving the perils of more than two months at sea, Peter Ruth and the other voyagers heard joyful cries from high above.[2] "The sailors from the mast see land," recorded David Scholtze. By noon, pilgrims standing on the main deck, gazing through fog, could make out land silhouetted on the horizon.

Their eager shouts would have awakened the senses of even the weariest of souls still below deck as they hurriedly scrambled topside to see for themselves. The main deck must have been abuzz with excitement as Peter and other travelers surely pointed their fingers over the rail and off in the distance, astounded by the navigational skill of the captain. After crossing nearly 3,500 miles of open sea, through wind and gale, directed only by the stars and some crude nautical instruments, he had hit his mark dead center.

Map of Delaware Bay showing Cape Henlopen and the towns of Lewes, Newcastle, and Philadelphia. Circa 1750. T. Kitchin, Public Domain via Wikimedia Commons. Enhanced and cropped to focus on the subject area.

From the dunes of Cape Henlopen, the first sight of sails on the horizon sent the river pilots of Lewes scrambling to their boats. Hurriedly launching them into the pounding surf, they rowed through the churning waves into the open ocean to hoist their sails. The race was on to see who would be the first to reach the inbound ship; the victor usually won a commission to navigate the treacherous waters of the Delaware River ahead. Beyond the sand bars, unpredictable currents, and narrow channels lay the port of Philadelphia.

As friendly winds carried their vessel closer to land, Naas recalled that from the main deck, he and the captain saw three boats sailing in.[3] "Our Captain took the second one and let the first and last return," added Scholtze.[4] Steadman recognized the second pilot from a previous voyage and took him at once aboard the ship.[5] According to Schultze, the captain planned to sail into the river the same night, and later, in the early evening, they entered the stream called the Delaware.[6]

The waters ahead were unnavigable but for the skill of an experienced river pilot. Around eight o'clock that night, just inside the mouth of the bay, there suddenly came a storm wind from the southwest worse than any before, explained Naas in a letter to his son Jacob. All had to help lower the sails and anchor for the first time at seven fathoms deep. The *Pennsylvania Merchant*, packed with a cargo of German immigrants from the Palatine region, stayed at anchor the whole night.[7]

The next morning, exhilaration surely surged through Peter, his wife Sophia, their four boys, and the other sojourners. For the first time since setting sail from England sixty-six days earlier, their vessel was hugged by land.

The entrance to the Delaware Bay, a seventeen-mile-wide stretch of water separating Delaware and New Jersey, was first discovered in 1609 by English explorer Henry Hudson. Thirty centuries before Europeans ever laid eyes on this continent, Native American tribes flourished in villages up and down the east coast of North America. How they originally came to this place on the continent is up for speculation. Mirroring the belief among most archeologists, historian Dick Carter writes that [ten] thousand years ago or longer, those first inhabitants were descendants of the early nomadic bands. They crossed the land bridge from Asia when ice covered the northern reaches of the continent and the seas were lower.[8]

Over several thousand years, those first Americans spread slowly across the face of the continent. Like their European intruders to follow, Native Americans waged war with one another over disputed territories. Two tribes eventually emerged in the east as they approached what is today Pennsylvania. Says Carter: The Lenape kept to the south, making their way into the Delaware Valley, while the Iroquois traveled north into New York and the Great Lakes region.[9] The Lenape who populated what is now lower Delaware were known as the Siconese.

By the time the travelers from the Palatine dropped anchor across the port-side rail, they could see, nestled at the southern tip of the great bay, a burgeoning anchorage called Lewes. Journalist Jennifer Ackerman writes "It was a good spot, a fertile highland just inside the elbow of Cape Henlopen on the Delaware Bay" and "a seafaring town since its birth, a port and harbor of refuge, home to ship carpenters, river pilots and fishermen." She further describes nearby marshes full of waterfowl and streams full of fish, turtles, otters, beaver, and muskrats, and that trees filled the land with thick forests of oak, walnut, hickory, and pine.[10]

The town itself lies across the beach and dunes, over a salt marsh, just on the other side of a tidal creek. It had been established little more than a hundred years earlier, in the spring of 1631, by the Dutch West India Company as a whaling and tobacco farming enterprise. According to Bob Kowtowski, writing in a journal of the Lewes Historical Society, a Dutch ship called the *Whale,* captained by Peter Heyes, deposited twenty-eight men on the shore, along with bricks, cattle, and other provisions.[11] He further wrote that the men built a brick dormitory and a cook house, surrounded by a wooden palisade, and had even begun cultivating the fields outside of their small stockade. Virginia Cullen, in her 1956 *History of Lewes, Delaware*, states that the place was called Zwaanendael, or Valley of the Swans, after flocks of these birds were seen floating on the creek.[12]

Unfortunately, for those early colonizers, misfortune would soon overtake enterprise. Within the first year, the settlement was destroyed and its inhabitants were massacred. It was believed to be the result of a dispute that began over the theft of a tin plate bearing the Dutch coat of arms.[13] One of the men who had been aboard the *Whale* in 1631—a man named David DeVries—had returned to Holland almost immediately after arriving to resupply the encampment. Shortly after his return home, news reached him about the fate of his embattled companions back in the Americas. A short time later, with a cargo hold full of trade goods, he set sail for Cape Henlopen to find out what happened to his ill-fated shipmates.

According to historian Harold B. Hancock:

DeVries arrived [back] at Swanendael, [where] he found the house and palisades burned. Scattered around the fields were the skulls and bones of the first settlers and their livestock. From a friendly Indian, DeVries learned what had happened.[14]

While there is considerable speculation about the validity of the Indian's account, here's what purportedly happened: One of the Siconese chiefs took the tin-plated Dutch coat of arms to make tobacco pipes, setting the deadly chain of events in motion. Because of the uproar among the Dutch colonizers over the theft, some of the Indians took it upon themselves to kill the offending chief. Other Indians, incensed by the death of their chief, then attacked and murdered the settlers.

If true, this is a classic example of a failure to communicate. De-Vries remained in the bay area for three months, bartering the trade goods he brought for precious animal pelts. After re-establishing peace with the Indians, he abandoned what remained of the doomed encampment for the last time. He set his course east, back to Holland, where his valuable cargo of animal furs would be fashioned into stylish articles of clothing.

Twenty-eight years later, in 1659, the Dutch West India Company returned to the territory they called New Netherlands to refortify the settlement for another attempt at colonization. The second Dutch settlement at Lewes, with a trading post and fort, attracted permanent settlers taking advantage of the protection of the fort.[15]

Two years earlier, in 1657, historian C. H. B. Turner writes, quoting a man named Alrich: "[It] is a fine and excellent country called the Whorekil, abounding very much in wild animals, birds, fish . . . and the land is so good and fertile that the like is nowhere to be found. It lies at the entrance of the Bay, about two leagues up from Cape Henlopen."[16]

Despite their successful recolonization effort, by 1674, the Dutch would relinquish possession of Delaware and much of America's northeast to England with the Treaty of Westminster—territory the Brits would hold until the Revolution ended their rule in 1783.

A full fifty years before that occurred, however, the Ruth family stood on the *Pennsylvania Merchant*'s main deck in that early fall of 1733, observing the unmistakable signs of European colonization on shore. Among the sites may have been tall sailing ships tied up at the dock just inside the inlet, or several small boats running aground on the beach with fishermen unloading the day's catch. At low tide, the townsfolk likely walked in the shallow tidal sand-flats, digging for clams with wooden sticks or multi-pronged rakes. Off in the distance, they may have even viewed wafting clouds of smoke from the brick chimney of a former tavern, now the home of Ryves Holt, naval officer of the port of Lewes.

Unknown to the Ruths and the other voyagers on the *Merchant* that morning, the threat posed on land by the Indians in those early days was not the colonist's only fear; danger would stalk them from the sea as well. Cape Henlopen, a natural breakwater that shields Lewes from the ocean's fury, was a perfect place for pirate ships to lie in wait. "In 1698, fifty well-armed men led by one, [Captain] Canoot, landed from a small sloop" and sacked Lewes, taking several townspeople hostage.[17] Two years later, the infamous Captain Kidd visited the Cape, enlisting the help of five enterprising Lewes citizens. Historian Hancock reports that several residents who "were suspected of being 'ould pirates' themselves—visited his ship and brought back goods for sale, unbeknownst to the [tax] collector of the port, Samuel Lowman."[18]

Nine years after that, Lewes was plundered in 1709 by one hundred men from a French privateer. The new Anglican rector, the Rev. William Black, wrote a letter to the Bishop of London saying, "This County of Sussex lyes so open to the Sea that there can be no safety in it." Later that year, he moved to the southern colony of Virginia.

Even the notorious Edward Teach, better known as Blackbeard, appeared in these parts in the summer of 1717.[19] Some said Blackbeard had a wife in Philadelphia and frequented a waterfront tavern there owned by a Swedish woman. Later that fall, the famed pirate plundered several merchant ships off Cape May, sparing only the one vessel filled with passengers.

By the time the Ruths reached Lewes, it had become a thriving coastal seaport. On the western side of the tidal creek lay Front Street-Pilot Town Road, a lane stretching some 80 perches long from end to end.[20] (As mentioned in Chapter 1, a perch is an old English unit of measurement equal to sixteen and a half feet.) Today, 80 perches would reach 440 yards—the length of nearly four and a half football fields. A land survey in 1723 shows that Front Street, which parallels Lewes Creek, extended the full width of the town.[21]

Historian Carter writes that in Lewes, "a culture grew up which was as close to and dependent on the sea as it was to the land. Many men spent years at sea before returning home to settle down to farming or tending store." During the 1720s, the town had a population estimated at about sixty families, maybe three hundred people in all, and its strategic location made it the center of Sussex County's universe. As a thriving town situated at the entrance to the Delaware Bay, it was the only place where pilots could be picked up to navigate vessels upstream to New Castle, Philadelphia, and beyond.[22]

Early transportation was also introduced between Lewes and Cape May, a New Jersey town perched on a sandy point at the top of the bay seventeen nautical miles north. Historian Turner reports that a "sail-boat or ferry" operated regularly between these two towns as early as 1660, carrying cargo and passengers between Delaware and New Jersey.[23] Perhaps some of the travelers and dry goods from Cape May were bound for the storefronts that dotted Front, South, and Ship Carpenter Streets. The general store in downtown Lewes, where they sold wheat milled into flour, as well as corn, tobacco, and various farming implements, would have been a hub for townsfolk and visitors alike. Sloops and shallops returning from Philadelphia filled the store's shelves with coffee, tea, hardware, rum, molasses, spices, imported cloth, and a great variety of products from the West Indies and Europe.[24] One street over, a smithy would surely have been hammering sizzling iron into horseshoes, hinges, cook pots, shovels, and hoes, while a variety of skilled tradesmen—carpenters, masons, shipwrights, tailors, and the like—

lived and worked in town as well. As for houses of worship, at least three congregations held services in Lewes, including the Church of England, the Presbyterian church, and the Quaker meeting house.

Just west of town, local farmsteads were scattered one mile or half a mile from one another, with the primary cash crops being wheat and tobacco, but also plentiful quantities of rye and corn.[25] Most farmers grew enough food to be self-sustaining, with the excess sold to buy manufactured luxuries. Almost every farmer kept a few cattle, hogs, oxen, and poultry, and after the harvest, they would haul their crops to Lewes for transport by shallop about ninety miles up the Delaware for sale in Philadelphia.

The exhausting work of tending land, animals, and crops was born by farmers alongside their families. Some had an indentured servant to help with the backbreaking labor, while a few of the wealthier farmers in the county owned slaves imported from nearby Maryland—the males working mostly in the fields while the women toiled inside as domestic servants. Rev. William Becket, the Anglican missionary at Lewes, concluded that there were only 241 black inhabitants in 1728 in all of Sussex County, including slaves and free blacks.[26]

Though it wasn't their final destination, that first sight of land on the horizon and the colonization of Lewes must have brought a collective sigh of relief to the travelers from the Palatine. However, that next morning, on the 25th of September, another newborn baby died. It was only after burying it in the river that their vessel departed once again.[27]

With seagulls likely looping overhead and wind in their sails, the crew soon put Lewes at their back. White sandy beaches and wetland marshes gave way to the lush green vegetation of wild grasses, trees, and shrubs scattered along a narrowing shoreline. "Here and there stood houses on the river bank" said Naas, "and fishing nets were hung upon the shores."

Pressing northwest, then due north, and finally northeast, they continued up the river. On September 26th, sixteen-year-old Scholtze told his diary that "a wind sprung up so we made good progress. All day people were coming on the vessel, bringing apples and peaches for sale"—only the voyagers' second taste of fresh fruit since leaving England nearly ten weeks earlier. "This rejoiced those who could lay hands on money."[28]

While it may be comforting to imagine that the majority of people onboard could afford a few pieces of fruit, the truth was that the toll for the journey to America was steep, even by twenty-first-century standards. A ticket for each adult passenger, called a "full freight," cost at least five British Pounds Sterling—just over $1,500 in US dollars today—for a voyage from England. (Children between the ages of four and fourteen were considered "half-freights" for calculating fares, and toddlers aged three and younger sailed without additional charge.) The Ruth family, at three and a half freights (two full freights, three half-freights, plus a two-year-old), would have paid at least $5,250 in inflation-adjusted dollars.

But the Ruth's voyage to America hadn't begun in England; they had carried the additional expense of traveling from their home in Germany to the port city of Rotterdam in the Netherlands—estimated to be about three pounds. Applying the same formula—three and a half freights—takes that leg of their land and river package to around $3,100 in today's money. All tolled, the cost for the Ruth family's journey to America, from Walhausen, Germany, to Philadelphia, Pennsylvania, would have been more than twenty-eight English pounds—$8,300 in today's dollars. That's about 280 days of wages (three-quarters of a year's pay) for a skilled tradesman in 1730—or the price of four horses or five cows.

Some of the pilgrims onboard the *Pennsylvania Merchant* were not as well off as the Ruths, however. They had to barter themselves for a contract of indentured servitude—a voluntary form of slavery that legally bound them to an employer for three to five years (or more) of labor upon their arrival—to pay the cost of passage. If they were lucky, the working conditions were tolerable. For others, voluntary servitude would prove to be harsh.

A third means of travel applied to the poorest of the pilgrims. These travelers could earn their passage "without requiring advance payment, either by cash or by signature on indentures. Passengers were allowed to arrange payment after they arrived in Philadelphia."[29] These new colonists, called "redemptioners," arranged for a collect-on-delivery form of indentured servitude. When the ship docked, if they were lucky, a local relative or friend might come forward to pay their fare. Most, however, were not so fortunate.

In these cases, the labor skills of the go-now, pay-later voyagers were auctioned off the dock to repay the shipping company for the cost of their passage. This arrangement placed them at great disadvantage. Since the conditions of their indenture were not worked out until after their arrival, they had little leverage in negotiating the provisions of their servitude. To further add to their distress, if their ship was set to sail before a deal was struck, they were "consigned to local merchants who collected the amounts due for their sale."[30] Thankfully, most redemptioners were consigned fairly quickly, according to pilgrim Naas's letter to his son. "I was amazed . . . about the young and strong people and artisans, how rapidly they are gone as masons, carpenters, and all other trades. Even old people with grown children who can do only farm work [are taken]."[31]

Fortunately, Peter, Sophia, and their sons did not have to indenture themselves to pay for their passage. Because the Ruths had been prosperous farmers and artisans back in the Palatine, they had reached a level of affluence that allowed Peter and his family to afford the cost of passage to America. Without supporting documentation, I am left to assume that Peter likely sold his farmland and the animals and equipment he used to cultivate it, along with selling or bartering most of their household items and other belongings they would have had to leave behind.

Back on the *Pennsylvania Merchant*—the second day of their journey after leaving Lewes, on the morning of the 27th of September—a heavy fog hung over the river as their brigantine sailed through the haze past New Castle, the young colony's capital. Still twenty-nine miles downriver from Philadelphia, the *Merchant* encountered local vendors once again on small boats offering one last "opportunity to procure apples and peaches." It is not known how many fortunate passengers had the spare change to enjoy them.

Despite the hefty cost—not only monetary, but physical and emotional as well—the Ruths and their Palatine companions were far from the only adventurous souls on the river seeking a new beginning in North America. Along their passage, they would have surely crossed other sailing ships heading south toward Lewes. The cargo they carried, people and freight, was bound for colonial ports to the north and south: New York, Boston, Charleston, and others. Some ventured even farther north to Nova Scotia, Quebec, and Newfoundland.

Other ships would have caught friendly winds heading hundreds of miles to the south, past the Florida peninsula to the West Indies. In the Caribbean, they would find markets eager for everything they grew, raised, and manufactured back home. Their cargo holds were filled with an assortment of grains, including wheat milled into flour from

Pennsylvania and Delaware farms, along with ham, pork, candles, and soap. They would have also transported lumber, poultry, cattle, and horses—things found in short supply on the islands. For the return trip, they would have stuffed the hollow bellies of their ships with rum, molasses, and sugar, setting a course north for the colonies.

Passenger vessels would also sail past Lewes into the open sea. With easterly winds puffing their sails, these ships would follow the stars toward the horizon, transporting human cargo back across the Atlantic to England and other ports on the European continent.

Only three days after departing from Lewes, on September 28, 1733, the *Pennsylvania Merchant*, with "very little wind," glided "with the flood-tide" into Philadelphia's burgeoning harbor and tied up at the city's public dock.[32] "Thanks and praise to the Lord for this blessing!" recorded Scholtze in his diary.[33] Theirs would be one of seven ships that year bringing German immigrants to this port. During the decade that followed, well over 60 percent of all immigrants arriving in Philadelphia were of German origin.

Simply reaching the port of Philadelphia from Lewes brought a unique set of challenges. Not only could it take anywhere from four to seven days to reach the city depending on shifting shoals, currents, and weather, but there was another major impediment: it was the only port south of Canada that was blocked by ice in the winter, sometimes for months on end.[34] Despite this, says Philadelphia historian Michael Schreiber, "ships and shippers came here by preference because it had the largest concentration of people in English-speaking America, including many with wealth and sophisticated tastes."

Depiction of Philadelphia harbor, late eighteenth century. "Arch Street Ferry" by William Russell Birch. Creative Commons CC0, via Wikimedia Commons.

Upon their jubilant arrival, the Ruths and their shipmates would have encountered peddlers who earned a living from the sea, along with shops filled with merchants who made rope, sails, and barrels. The streets teemed with stevedores, smithies, riggers, chandlers, wheelwrights, and other maritime traders. And, of course, there were the waterfront taverns. Just beyond all of that stood the courthouse and market square where, on Wednesdays and Saturdays, merchants would hawk their wares—hens, chickens, wildfowl, butchered beef, fruits, and vegetables.

Geographically located to maximize commerce in colonial America, Philadelphia benefited from the climate in the surrounding rural counties, which was perfect for growing wheat. When milled into flour, the white powdery grain expanded the city's role as an economic power-house, as much of the city's grain was exported throughout the British Empire and beyond.

Depiction of the Old Courthouse at Market Square, Circa 1750.
Artist unknown – Creative Commons CC0, via Wikimedia Commons.

Other commodities also helped bolster Philadelphia as a commercial hub. Tobacco emerged as a staple in Pennsylvania's export trade, with the colony exporting well over a million pounds in four years in the early 1700s—the majority coming from the three lower Delaware counties.[35] Furs and skins of beaver, mink, fox, and other animals were traded for manufactured goods, then loaded onto ships to England and mainland Europe, where the fur was converted into hats and luxury clothing.

As in any newly adopted country, pilgrims had to acclimate to the law of the land. The Ruth family and the other Palatines found a government run by Englishmen, which meant English common law was the authority. As foreign-speaking immigrants accustomed to other forms of government flocked to the area, concerns grew about their loyalty to the Crown of England. To allay these fears, the Provincial Council enacted a loyalty oath in 1727. Within two years, the oath was expanded to include loyalty and fidelity to the proprietor of the province: William Penn.

The day after landing, Scholtze recorded in his journal: "We were obliged to go to the Court-House and take our oath of allegiance to the King."[36] According to the State of Pennsylvania's *Minutes of the Provincial Council of Pennsylvania*: Standing before "the Honourable . . . Lt. Governor and Several of the Magistrates," the Provincial Council proceedings show "sixty seven Palatines" signed the declaration "who with their Families, making in all One hundred eighty seven Persons." They "were imported here in the Briganteen Pennsylvania Merchant, of London, [Captain] John Stedman, Mr., from Rotterdam, but last from Plymouth."[37]

These minutes, later published in 1840, list Peter Ruth's name as Pieter Roodt. However, in his 1934 book *Pennsylvania German Pioneers*, Ralph Beaver Strassburger describes three different passenger lists, all containing Peter Ruth's name.[38] The first was supposed to be completed by the ship's captain but was often "prepared carelessly," says Strassburger. Captain Steadman's list shows his name as Pieter Roodt. (Family genealogist Anna Ruth Salzman suggests that the German name Ruth must have sounded like Roodt to the Dutch Captain.) The second list was created for passengers who were well enough that day to sign the oath of allegiance, and list number three was for those who signed the oath of abjuration, which renounced allegiance to their former country. The allegiance and abjuration lists show Peter's name as Peter ℗ Roodt.

The Ⓟ indicates he signed with a mark—a large "P." It is not known who signed the words "Peter" and "Roodt" on either side of the mark.

While only Peter and the other adult males over age sixteen were required to sign the loyalty declaration, the names of their wives and children were also recorded in the provincial records at the Philadelphia courthouse that day. As for their shipboard companions, these newly minted Americans disembarked from the *Pennsylvania Merchant* for the last time and disappeared anonymously into Philadelphia's 7,000-plus inhabitants. They, along with the Ruth family, each set out to pursue their American dreams.

CHAPTER FOUR

The Settling: Pennsylvania Dutch Country

With their sons Michael, Jacob, Christian, and Peter at their side, Peter and Sophia headed west, leaving the safety and relative comfort of Philadelphia for a destination some sixty miles distant—a place called Sinking Spring in the Dutch country of Pennsylvania.

Of the various factors that influenced Peter to leave his homeland, a Quaker named William Penn was surely one of them. After acquiring more than 40,000 square miles of territory in 1681 from King Charles II of England, Penn needed to populate his colony in the New World.[1] The territory included all lands between Maryland and New York west of the Delaware River. The purchase was "in liquidation of a debt of 16,000 pounds which the British crown owed to Penn's father."

In today's dollars, £16,000 would be about $4,522,621—only $113.06 per square mile, or less than eighteen cents per square acre. (In 2022, according to the US Department of Agriculture, the average sale price of one acre of Pennsylvania cropland is about $8,300.) A year later, Penn was also deeded what is now the state of Delaware.

An Englishman by birth, Penn visited the central Rhine region in 1677. Aware of the political and religious turmoil plaguing the Palatines, Penn arranged his trip to "extend the principles and the organization of the Society of Friends in two countries . . . Holland and Germany."[2] After his vast North American land acquisition, Penn printed thousands of pamphlets promoting the virtues of his colony in Pennsylvania. His emissaries were charged with distributing them throughout the left bank of the Rhine.

"Short as that journey was," said University of Pennsylvania professor Oswald Seidensticker on December 10, 1877, "it had a very potent influence on the settlement of Pennsylvania, preparing the way for an immigration that rapidly filled the wooded hills and fertile valleys of the young colony."[3] The pamphlet Penn's agents distributed to Rhinelanders depicted a "Holy Experiment," offering religious freedom and political liberty to those who accepted his proposal—and thousands did.

This promise of the separation of church and state—in contrast to Germany where "the Church and State were one"[4]—along with the favorable reports from Peter's sister-in-law Susanna, who was already in America, surely added to the allure of the New World.

Over two centuries after the Ruths arrived, John Lowry Ruth declared: "Picture with me, this little group standing open-eyed and bewildered in a new strange country with tiny settlements far apart in the midst of virgin forests with no roads or paths except Indian trails."[5]

Heading out of Philadelphia, the Ruth family likely followed the Perkiomen Path, an old Indian trail leading to Reading. The Indians seized every advantage offered by the terrain, fashioning narrow footpaths to carry moccasined men and women along trails cut through pristine forests, beside creeks or rivers, and along ridges.[6]

The path Peter, Sophia, and the boys traversed crossed the Schuylkill River—a four- or five-mile hike from there led them to their new home near Sinking Spring.

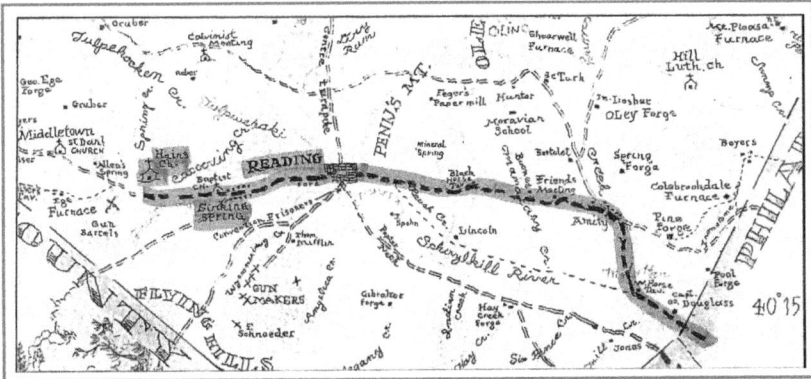

1776 Berks County map drawn by J. R. Rowe. The shaded area shows the route the Ruths traveled on the Perkiomen Path leading from Philadelphia to Reading, Sinking Spring, and Hain's Church. Also shown, but not shaded, are the Schuylkill River and the Cacoosing and Tulpehaucken Creeks. The map was enhanced and cropped to about 15 percent of its original size to focus on the subject area.

Family historian John Lowry Ruth wrote that Peter was granted a patent by the proprietary Penns on a small tract of land, which he called "Half-Moon." There he "erected his home, cleared the land, tilled the soil, and through untiring industry gained the rewards that follow."[7] (Interestingly, British explorer Henry Hudson's ship was named *Half Moon*. I don't know if Peter was a student of history or knew of Hudson's exploration of North America, but even if it was a mere coincidence, Peter's first homestead bore the same name.) While the exact number of homes Peter built is unknown, Half Moon was probably the first of several, including the old stone house along Cacoosing Creek that

Kathy and I visited—and that I fell in love with—during our reunion weekend in 1983.

Lucky for the Ruths, they weren't completely alone in their new surroundings. Three years earlier, Sophia's sister Susanna (Lauer) Theiss and her husband, Jon, had come to Pennsylvania by way of Philadelphia on a ship called the *Thistle*. Sophia's half-brother, Christian Lauer, a blacksmith, had come to America with Peter and Sophia on the *Pennsylvania Merchant*. Susanna, Christian, and the rest of the Lauer clan settled near Tulpehocken Creek, some ten-plus miles northwest of the Ruth family homestead. Undoubtedly, there were numerous family gatherings between the Ruths and their good friends from the old country, and this extended family likely provided some of the labor to establish their first homestead.

The Ruths and their neighbors from the Palatine came from small villages where farming was a revered profession. The cultural attitudes and practices these German immigrants brought from the old country transformed Pennsylvania's agricultural practices and would become the prototype for America's future agricultural development.[8]

But life in the Pennsylvania Dutch country offered some additional challenges to the usual rigors of farm life. When Europeans first settled in Pennsylvania, more than 98 percent of the land they found was covered in forest. In a virgin territory, the Ruths had to fell the surrounding trees to flatten the woodlands and transform the forest into farmland. This punishing work was done by hand and ax, toppling each tree with exhausting repetition, then clearing the underbrush. And unlike their English counterparts, German farmers removed the stumps, making the fertile ground easier to plow and the land more productive.

The fallen timber was fashioned into logs for the Ruths and other settlers to build their first primitive homes and barns. Extra wood was split for firewood or cut into longer rails for fencing. They tilled the land by walking behind a horse or ox, dragging a metal-bladed, wooden plow that sliced through the hard soil in straight rows. After tilling the pristine earth, compacted mostly with decayed leaves and rotted wood, they planted the seeds by hand and harvested their bounty by walking through the crop rows, swinging a sickle through the stalks.

German farmers routinely rotated their crops on three- or four-year cycles to restore the fertility of worn-out soil. The first crops were usually wheat and hay, followed in the next years by oats, buckwheat, or corn. In the final year they planted clover. After the clover was plowed, they sowed new crop seeds to begin the cycle again.

For Germans, the care shown for their animals and crops stemmed from their belief that agriculture was not merely a way to make a living but a way of life. Each family worked their farming enterprise as a well-organized production. Sharon A. Brown, in a study she prepared for the National Park Service, said:

[They] further distinguished from their neighbors by the care they provided their livestock. Barns and stables sheltered cows, horses, sheep and hogs. Animals were not allowed to roam freely or forage. Large trees were sometimes retained in pastures to provide shade for animals and . . . fields were being fenced to keep stock from wandering. Oxen were used as draft animals, sheep provided wool for home spinning, hogs supplied meat . . . and milk cows were the source of milk and cheese. Poultry, of course, supplied families with eggs.[9]

One key advantage of the land they settled was the nearby Cacoosing Creek, which offered an endless supply of fresh drinking water for the Ruths and their farm animals. They also used the Creek to irrigate the meadow by building dams and running the water through irrigation ditches or small canals.[10] In fact, every aspect of farm life for these pioneers from the Palatine appeared to be orchestrated to maximize function and gain optimal results. National Park Service writer Brown put it this way:

> Common features of eastern Pennsylvania's [German] colonial farmsteads included the site of the dwelling being located near a spring; a road separating the house from the barn; the garden being located at the front or rear doors; and the orchard, generally containing apple trees, being planted on a slope near buildings. A pig sty was generally between the house and barn . . . and the house's living room was oriented toward the sun. Barns were located so that barnyard drainage would flow into, and fertilize, meadows.

Numerous documents reveal the new immigrants were good stewards of their land and property, viewing their farms as legacies to be handed down to the next generation. As such, the Ruths and their neighbors from the fatherland acquired a reputation for frugality, industry, hard work, sobriety, and stability.

As one would expect, the hardships of frontier farm life were not confined solely to men. Wives and daughters milked cows, gathered eggs from hen houses, and plucked fruit from trees in the orchard. They baked bread, churned butter, and made cheese while planting gardens and canning fruits and vegetables. Women were also responsible for all the knitting, spinning, weaving, sewing, and mending. In their "spare" time, they cooked meals, washed dirty laundry, birthed babies, and looked after children. For the Ruths and other German families in the colony of Pennsylvania, long days started before the sun came up and didn't end until well after it disappeared below the horizon.

With shared experience, heritage, and religion, the immigrants from the Palatine bonded over a common longing for friendship, companionship, worship, and protection.[11] While their farmsteads were often far apart, their very existence and subsistence bound them together into a community—and the church played a big role in that. Church records show the first German Palatines to reach the area arrived in the spring of 1723, and by 1728, thirty-three families lived there. Five years later, the Ruth family and others added to that number. (The largest portion of settlers belonged to the Protestant German Reformed and German Lutheran churches, while smaller numbers adhered to the pacifistic Mennonite, Amish, and Brethren faiths."[12])

The origins of the Reformed Church go back to the Reformation in the sixteenth century when rogue German Catholic priest Martin Luther and his counterpart in Switzerland, Ulrich Zwingli, rebelled against the Catholic church. Other reformers like John Calvin emerged at the same time—Calvin's theology became bedrock for Presbyterians and what would become the various offshoots of the Reformed Church movement, setting them apart from the followers of Luther. Lutherans hold that anyone can attain salvation through faith alone, while Calvinists, who believe in predestination, God's grace and salvation are granted only to the chosen few.

The German Reformed Church that emerged in Peter's fatherland set a new confessional standard for churches in the Palatine. Based on the Heidelberg Catechism published in 1563, this new standard specified three separate sections for its followers: The first part recognizes the depravity of mankind, acknowledging that humans are enslaved to sin at birth. The second piece states that redemption is only possible through Jesus Christ. The final segment is expressed through the example of living a holy or godly life.

The early Reformed Church, known for its conservative doctrine, now includes Protestant churches, from Presbyterians to the United Church of Christ and various other Christian Reformed churches. Even the United Methodist Church has roots leading back to the Heidelberg Catechism.

Hain's Reformed Church was a vital part of Peter and Sophia's life from the beginning, and they quickly became prominent members of their congregation. But less than two years after their arrival in Sinking Spring, tragedy struck. On the 30th of May, 1735, Sophia died. Historical records surrounding her death are contradictory, leaving unanswered questions; however, the most likely cause was the birthing of her daughter, Anna Catharine.

Regardless of the circumstances surrounding Sophia's death, five years later, on the first of August, 1740, Peter married a twenty-five-year-old Berks County woman named Catharine Meyer (Mayer). (One source indicates that Peter's marriage to Catharine occurred as early as 1736.) Catharine had also emigrated from Germany, six years after Peter and Sophia's arrival. She had sailed from Europe on the *Friendship*, arriving in Philadelphia in 1739 with her brother and his family, joining three other brothers who had previously settled along the Tulpehocken Creek in Berks County. Historian Cyrus Fox writes that Peter was a prosperous farmer of Heidelberg on the Cacoosing Creek, and that with his new wife Catharine, he held a leading position in the social and general interests of the vicinity.[13]

Though Catharine was thought to be a Lutheran when she arrived in America, she joined Peter as a member of the Hain's Reformed Church after their marriage. During that time—in the years between 1730 and 1757—the congregants depended on lay pastors to preach the gospel and the tenets of the Heidelberg Catechism. In their church history book, W.J. Kershner and Adam Lerch write:

The Reformed Church then had only a few ministers, and those adhering to the Reformed faith were scattered over a great extent of territory, with no roads communicating or making places accessible other than trails or only partly opened roads through dense forests.[14]

In those early days, services were held in the houses and barns of parishioners. But on December 1, 1752, George Hain deeded four acres of land in Heidelberg township to Peter and four others as trustees for constructing a church building and a cemetery. (It is uncertain when the first log church was built, but church records reveal the congregation erected a stone church building of large dimensions as early as 1766.) In what is now Wernersville, Hain's Reformed Church sat atop a "prominent hill-top overlooking the country for miles around, as if keeping guard over the hearts and homes over which she looks."

By 1752, 60 percent of the entire population of Pennsylvania was of German origin—and Peter had great influence in Sinking Spring. Family historian Anna Ruth Salzman uncovered that the land on which the town of Sinking Spring is located was once the sole property of the Ruth family,[15] land holdings that were confirmed as "ground zero" for the Ruth family by Tom Gerhart, long-time president of the Pennsylvania German Society.

But despite living in America for almost thirty years and acquiring nearly 900 acres of land, Peter and his German-born sons were not "natural born" subjects of the Crown of England. Although Peter signed a loyalty oath when he arrived in Philadelphia in 1733, that pledge of allegiance did not come with a grant of citizenship. The official privilege of English law and liberty was conferred only upon its citizens.

In pursuance of an act of parliament during the reign of King George, foreign-born Protestants settling in America had two conditions to meet before citizenship would be granted: 1) residency of seven years, without being absent for longer than two months, at any one time; and 2) taking the Sacrament of the Lord's Supper in a Protestant or Reformed Congregation in their province within the prior three months. Completing these two stipulations entitled them to became natural-born subjects of Great Britain.[16]

On April 10, 1761, Peter, with sons Michael and Jacob, traveled to Philadelphia where they were naturalized by the Supreme Court. Hain's Church archives confirm that all three declared before the court that they had last taken the Sacraments of the Holy Communion on March 15th of that year."[17]

Surrounded by family and wrapped snugly in the protective cocoon of a close-knit German community, the Ruths were seemingly insulated from the world around them. Life in eastern Pennsylvania along the Cacoosing Creek was good. But ominous storm clouds were gathering on the other side of the Blue Mountains, and the tempestuous winds of change were blowing in their direction.

Between 1681 and 1753, a fragile peace had existed on the frontier between America's original inhabitants and the early European settlers. The Covenant Chain—a series of alliances and treaties created mainly for trade with the Five Iroquois Nations (Mohawk, Onondaga, Oneida, Cayuga, and Seneca), helped ensure peaceful coexistence in the British colonies. Additionally, Penn's sons negotiated two land sales, which further solidified the peace during this time.

The Five Nations of the Iroquois trace their roots back to the late sixteenth century. This tribal federation, or league, was formed partly to promote peace by ending the needless bloodshed between warring tribes who shared a common or similar language. Due to its sheer size, their alliance was a formidable and intimidating fighting force that could be used to attack or fend off hostile tribes to the north, south, and west. (In 1722, the league expanded to Six Nations, with the addition of the Tuscarora tribe who migrated north into Pennsylvania and New York.) To address grievances against individual members or other tribes, the league held a constitutional form of governance—one of the basic tenets of which was the separation of tribal civil affairs from their various religious beliefs, or the separation of church and state.

The Native Americans were fascinated by eighteenth-century European customs, tools, and technology and seemed eager to trade their land for things they could not produce themselves. The first such sale, according to historian Fox, took place on September 7, 1732. The deed shows the consideration exchanged by the Penns consisted of "20 brass kettles . . . 100 blankets . . . 60 linen shirts, 20 hats, 6 made coats, 12 pair of shoes and buckles, 30 pairs of stockings, 300 lbs. of gun powder, 600 pounds of lead, 20 fine guns . . . 50 tomahawks . . . 50 planting hoes" plus knives, tobacco, flints, paint, ribbons, rings, tobacco pipes, and more.[18] All of this was in addition to "20 gallons of rum and 50 pounds in money."

The second land sale occurred seventeen years later, on August 22, 1749. Documents show that the deal was an all-cash transaction paid with 500 British Pounds Sterling. By then, the Indians had learned the value and benefit of currency as a trading commodity. (The 1749 land sale for £500 would be about $131,585 in today's US dollar. The earlier sale in 1732 for £50 would amount to about $14,387, paid in addition to the various trade goods.) These acquisitions from the Indians granted Penn vast expanses of land west of Philadelphia, including all of Berks County. The deed says explicitly: "All those tracts of land lying on or near the River Schuylkill . . . [and] any of the branches, streams, fountains or springs thereof, eastward or westward . . . [including] the waters or streams of which flow into or toward the said river Schuylkill." The document further describes ". . . all land whatsoever lying within the said bounds; and between the branches of Delaware River, on the eastern side of the said land, and the branches or streams running into the River Susquehanna, on the western side of the said land." While the language in the two deeds is rather specific, some historians believe the Indians thought Penn's land acquisition deal was more of a shared usage arrangement established for hunting and trading purposes rather than an outright land sale.

Through the first quarter of the eighteenth century, the Covenant Chain continued to hold the fragile peace together. For the two and a half decades that followed—those leading up the French and Indian War—the tenuous harmony binding the two diverse cultures was largely due to the efforts of a German immigrant from the Palatine named Conrad Weiser. According to Joseph S. Walton in his book on Weiser: "He was [the] one man who, during these difficulties, retained the confidence of both the Iroquois and the Southern Indians," as well as the colonial governments.[19]

As a sixteen-year-old, Weiser lived with the Mohawk Indians for eight months during the winter and spring of 1712–1713. Learning to speak their language, he gained intimate familiarity with their unique customs and culture. He also experienced firsthand the hardships of Indian life, especially their dreadful struggles for survival during the bitter winter months. The awareness Weiser gained from this childhood encounter would prove invaluable to the mid-Atlantic colonies, especially Pennsylvania during the French and Indian War.

Between 1731 and 1756 Weiser negotiated numerous land purchases, treaties, and peace accords between the Six Iroquois Nations—sometimes called the Iroquois League—the troublesome Delawares, and the colonial governments in Pennsylvania, Maryland, and Virginia. His diplomatic efforts helped to keep the nations of the Iroquois League aligned with the British in the French and Indian War. Because of this, the Colonies would face primarily the Delawares and Canadian Iroquois, not the entire Iroquois League. If the British colonies had faced all six Iroquois Nations, as well as the Delaware Indians, the tide of the war could have tilted to the French and the course of world history may have been forever altered.

Known as the Seven Years' War in Europe, the French and Indian War (1754–1763) would change the delicate balance between the colonies and the Indians. Historian Cyrus T. Fox writes:

> The English and French were at war over the rights of who should possess a vast domain now known as the Mississippi Valley and the Middle West, including the Great Northwest Territory. The English claimed it by reason of having first settled on the shores of the Atlantic and the French because of her possessing Canada and Louisiana.[20]

About two million settlers were in the American colonies then, while only about 60,000 people occupied the vast French territories. To have any chance for victory, the outnumbered French needed the support of a formidable ally—and they found one in the dispossessed Native Americans. The French promised to help them drive the British settlers out of Indian lands and back to their ships. On the larger world stage, this was a power struggle between England and France for control of the North American continent, and global supremacy between the world's two superpowers.

By 1750, most Indians along the east coast and throughout Pennsylvania had already moved west and north, far beyond the Blue Mountains—always trying to stay ahead of the advancing settlers. The war brought them back, though, with frequent Indian raids up and down the frontier from New York to Virginia. Warriors with faces and bodies painted black, and eagle feathers dangling from their hair, launched surprise attacks against unsuspecting settlers. "They didn't have the power of overwhelming force," writes David Venditta, but "stealth, speed and the element of surprise gave them the advantage."[21]

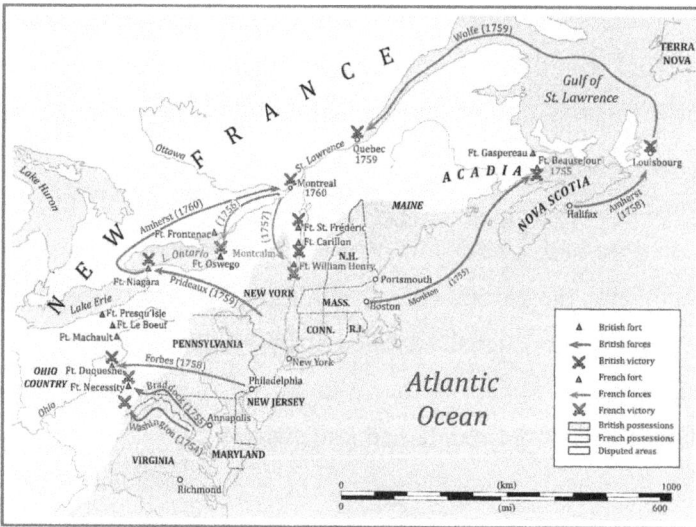

French and Indian War map showing British possessions along the east coast as well as land claimed by the French and the disputed territory. Map by Hoodinski under Creative Commons Attribution-Share Alike 3.0 Unported.

The first attack in Pennsylvania against white settlers occurred on October 16, 1755, at Penn's Creek in Union County, nearly sixty miles northwest of Sinking Spring. Two and a half months later in Philadelphia, on the 29th of December, a report was submitted to Pennsylvania Governor Robert Morris. Presented by the Secretary to the Provincial Council, the report declared:

> During all this month the Indians have been burning and destroying all before them in the County of Northampton, and have already burnt fifty houses here, and murdered above one hundred Persons, and are still continuing their Ravages, Murders, and Devastations, and have actually overrun and laid waste a great part of that County.

By April 8, 1756, little more than three months later, events had become so worrisome that Governor Morris enacted the Scalp Act, calling for bounties to be paid for taking either Indian prisoners or their scalps. Historian George Bray says that while Europeans did not originate scalping, they did encourage its spread through the establishment of bounties.[22] The price for Indian scalps was pegged at $130 for warriors, and $50 for Native American women. Higher rewards were paid for taking prisoners: the provincial government offered $150 for Indian braves and $130 for their squaws.

Although scalping was considered barbaric by European standards of warfare, the governor's action was taken for several reasons. Beyond mere retaliation, terror was an effective psychological weapon: scalping Indians sent a clear message back to their foes. Strategically, there were other reasons as well. The practice encouraged bounty hunters to engage and kill their brutal enemy. It was also thought to be an effective way to count the number of Indians killed.

Later, that method of counting dead enemy combatants proved to be troublesome. It was discovered that many of the bounty hunters cut their scalps into several pieces to multiply their cash reward. Additionally, according to Bray, while most scalping victims died from their wounds, some of those left for dead lived—maybe to fight again or at least tell the story of their gruesome attack.

News of the Penn's Creek and Northampton County attacks undoubtedly reached the settlers in the Reading area. Only weeks after those attacks, in early November of 1755, it was reported that the Delawares killed or captured settlers along the Tulpehocken Creek in Berks County, fewer than ten miles away.[23] The Ruths and their neighbors must have been terrified.

When the Ruths first settled, the area along the Cacoosing Creek had long been a frequent stop for Indians on their way to their fishing and hunting grounds along the Schuylkill.[24] According to historian Cyrus Fox, the Indians camped among the homesteads and were free to help themselves to garden vegetables and the apples of the orchard. "They spread their table on the ground anywhere, and eat twice a day, morning and evening."[25] St. John's (Hain's) Church historians Kershner and Lerch further state that "the Palatines and the Germans always treated the Indians with strict adherence to honesty and never took advantage of them, and for this reason, there is no record of an Indian massacre in this section." This "speaks remarkably well for the early settlers and their peaceable disposition."[26]

Logic and fact challenge this rosy scenario, however. Berks County historian Fox contradicts their statement about the absence of Indian massacres in the area, saying that occasional murders occurred as late as 1763 near Sinking Spring. "John Fincher, his wife, and two sons were killed and one daughter carried away by the red-skinned enemy."[27] During this same murderous raid, says Fox, Nicholas Miller's wife and four children were killed, and two more children went missing. After reading both accounts, my guess is that it was probably more good fortune than neighborliness that kept the Ruths and other nearby families safe from Indian attacks.

One thing is sure: The native attackers from the north and west were bent on delivering fear, death, and destruction to all the interlopers who occupied Indian lands. And, many colonists were not as lucky as the Ruth family and some of their neighbors along the Cacoosing Creek.

On October 8, 1763, about forty miles northeast of Sinking Spring near what is now North Whitehall Township, a blacksmith named Ulrich Showalter saw Indians approaching. (Showalter was my fifth great-grandfather and later fought for America's independence in the Revolution.) Working on the roof of a building above the Lehigh River, off in the distance "twelve in all were seen wading across the river, a short distance above Siegfried's Bridge. . . . The greater part of the township was at the time still covered with dense forests, so that the Indians could go from one place to another in a straight line, through the woods, without being seen."[28]

Reaching the farm of John Mickley, the Indians spotted three of his children under a tree gathering chestnuts. When the children saw them approaching, they ran toward the woods. The youngest, Barbary, was seven and was overtaken almost immediately "by an Indian, who knocked her down with a tomahawk." Henry was nine and able to reach the fence, but as he was climbing, a tomahawk struck him in the back, which "instantly killed him." Both children were scalped. Eleven-year-old Peter, however, was able to make it to the woods, narrowly escaping his siblings' fate by hiding in the underbrush. Through the trees, off in the distance, he could hear the screams of the Schneider family, the next victims of the bloodthirsty attack. A short time later, he took off in the opposite direction and "ran with all his might" to his older brother's house, "to whom he communicated the melancholy intelligence."

Alarmed by news of the nearby Indian attacks, Peter Ruth and twenty-four other citizens of the county formed a militia. They wrote Governor Morris requesting military supplies in the form of arms and ammunition to protect themselves and their families. Fortunately for the Ruths and the other settlers, the danger posed by the merciless Indians passed without further incident, and the long, bloody struggle for control of North America finally ended with the Treaty of Paris on February 10, 1763. The French surrendered virtually all the Americas to England, ending the war for the colonies, but leaving in its wake as many as 10,000 dead on both sides, presumably half of them from sickness and disease.

The defeat of France, however, did not entirely end hostilities between Native Americans and settlers. Unfortunately for pioneers like the Mickley family, in some quarters, Indian attacks persisted for several years.

Only eight and a half years after the Treaty of Paris, on September 14, 1771, Peter Ruth drew his last breath. Having spent thirty-eight years in America, he was thought to be about seventy years of age. He had fathered fourteen children with two wives, and he had raised them in a God-fearing home that embraced the German values of thrift, honesty, hard work, faith, and family. But perhaps even more extraordinary is that he had also been the father of an American legacy, one whose roots not only run deep in the Dutch country of Pennsylvania, but whose branches would stretch far and wide into the soul of America for centuries to come.

Peter's first wife Sophia is believed to be buried in the "Old Churchyard" at Tulpehocken Trinity United Church of Christ, about fourteen miles west of their home, but the final resting place for Peter and Catharine is unknown. Some believe they are buried together at St.

John's (Hain's) Reformed Church in Wernersville; however, church records do not list their names among the graves. Others, like Tom Gerhart of the Pennsylvania German Society, believe they could be buried in a private cemetery or at one of the other Reformed churches in Berks or Lebanon counties. Regardless of their final resting place, though, one thing is sure: these pioneering ancestors will never be forgotten.

Soon after Peter's death, distant thunderclouds would begin to roll across the horizon. The foreboding winds of change were again gusting, and the seemingly peaceful Cacoosing Creek was in its path. This time, the blustering gusts blew from the east, on a faraway island across the Atlantic Ocean.

CHAPTER FIVE

The Revolution: Life, Liberty, and the Pursuit

y the time the first shots rang out at Lexington, the Ruths had been in America for forty-two years. Peter's eight sons and at least three grandsons, along with several of his sons-in-law and family patriots from other branches of our extended clan, joined them in the fight for independence from the tyranny of English rule. As far as the Revolution was concerned, the Ruth family was all in.

According to James Fritz in his book about the Pennsylvania Dutch, "The coming American Revolution would allow the so-called church Germans to step forward as patriots to fight for independence from England."[1] However, not all German-Americans would follow the lead of the Ruth clan. Support for the war among German immigrants seemed to center along religious lines as the Quakers, Amish, Mennonites, and other pacifist orders were loyalists and vocal opponents of the break from England. In contrast, Lutherans and Reformed church members like the Ruths were solidly on the patriot side. After all, they had come to Pennsylvania to escape political oppression on the European continent. They would not tolerate it in America.

America's struggle for independence from British rule started long before the shooting began. Numerous Parliamentary Acts and incidents of injustice led to America's rebellion against the Crown. Sifting through old historical documents, I came across an edition of the *Pennsylvania Packet* dated April 24, 1781, six years after the opening salvos at Lexington. The front page featured this eighteenth-century version of a letter to the editor:

> I am a plain, honest countryman, and [I own] a small farm.
> To the PRINTER . . . My neighbours all round say, the taxes are very high—so they are says I—[But] neighbours, when we first began to fight the [King's] regulars, we promised to spend our lives and our fortunes, before we would submit to them . . . I am willing to give up a quarter, half, or the whole of my estate, and my life too, sooner than I would suffer the king of England to take it away as he pleases, [or] stop our town meetings, pick our juries, make all of our laws, choose our governors, councellors and judges, shut up our ports, [and obstruct] our trade . . . [The King sends] his soldiers and hirelings to England that they might not be hanged for murdering us . . . [And then they] carry us there to be hanged when his governor pleases.[2]

This patriot's letter succinctly captured why ordinary Americans—natural-born and immigrant alike—were willing to fight and die for their independence. These sentiments clearly resonated with the Ruth clan, as over twenty-five of my ancestors fought for the cause of liberty in the American Revolution. What follows are the accounts of four of these family patriots.

It was April 19, 1775, when the early-warning system set up by the colonials brought Massachusetts militias and Minute Men to Lexington and Concord. According to several historical sources, two of those responding to the Lexington Alarm were my fifth great-grandfather, William and Sarah Robinson's eldest son, Elijah, and my fifth great-granduncle, Eliphalet Hyde, the son of Elijah and Ruth Hyde.

The night before, two lanterns flickered briefly from the steeple of the Old North Church in Boston. The signal, "one if by land, two if by sea," alerted patriots that the Redcoats were moving toward Concord, rowing across the harbor in boats rather than marching by land. This signal sent Paul Revere and William Dawes on their famous rides at about ten o'clock that evening. As they galloped through the surrounding towns, other riders joined, alerting the local citizenry. With church bells ringing and gunfire sounding the alarm, Minute Men grabbed their weapons and headed for town greens, followed by the rest of the militia. By the time the British crossed the water, word of their imminent arrival had already reached Lexington and Concord,[3] and the element of surprise for the British was lost.

With the objective of seizing a cache of patriot weapons and ammunition stockpiled at Concord, about 700 British Regulars set off from Boston that night.[4] At around five o'clock in the morning, the Redcoats reached Lexington. Waiting for them was Captain John Parker's assemblage of seventy or more militia and Minute Men.

There on the village green, the Patriots and Redcoats faced off, each side shouting taunts and jeers at the other. Amid the confusion and without warning, a shot rang out.[5] It is uncertain which side pulled the first trigger, but a melee ensued. When the smoke cleared, eight

Americans lay dead, with a similar number injured. One redcoat was reported wounded.

Leaving Lexington behind, the British marched on to nearby Concord. At the town's North Bridge, they encountered stiff resistance from 300 to 400 patriots. Gunfire rang out, leaving two colonists dead and three redcoats mortally wounded.

Poet Ralph Waldo Emerson later immortalized the clash at the North Bridge in his 1837 "Concord Hymn." The opening stanza reads:

By the rude bridge that arched the flood/
Their flag to April's breeze unfurled/
Here once the embattled farmers stood/
And fired the shot heard round the world.

Depiction of the Battle of Lexington in 1775. Oil on canvas was painted by William Barnes Wollen in 1910. Public Domain, via Wikimedia Commons.

In the aftermath, the British beat a hasty retreat back to their home base in Boston, suffering numerous casualties along the way in skirmishes with colonial militiamen and Minute Men. The American Revolution had begun.[6]

While it is fascinating to contemplate that two of my ancestors answered the Lexington Alarm on the opening days of the Revolution, historical records from the Revolutionary War period are rife with conflicting and sometimes mistaken information, and only Eliphalet Hyde's participation is verifiable.

Under the command of Captain James Clark, on April 22, 1775, Eliphalet and some seventy citizen soldiers marched out of Lebanon, Connecticut, bound for Lexington, Massachusetts.[7] A Connecticut Historical Society publication reveals Corporal Hyde received wages for eighteen days of service for his Lexington Alarm participation, involvement that is further confirmed in a handwritten report submitted by Captain James Clark, dated July 12, 1775.[8]

Elijah Robinson's service record, on the other hand, persists as questionable. Historian William R. Cutter's genealogical reference book, *New England Families*, shows that Elijah served in the Lexington Alarm,[9] a claim also reported under the listing for Elijah in the online genealogy service, *Find-A-Grave*. (The contributor who maintains Elijah's listing there told me she acquired the Lexington Alarm reference from Cutter's book.) Nearly six years after the Lexington Alarm, Elijah also served fifteen days when the 4th Suffolk County Regiment was mustered on March 3, 1781. Under the command of Major General Lincoln, they marched to Rhode Island.[10] The epitaph chiseled on Elijah's gravestone records his service in the 4th Suffolk County Regiment, seemingly affirming Cutter's reference.

Family historian Mary Parsons, however, throws a wet blanket on the accuracy of the above accounts. She notes that six Elijah/Elisha Robinsons are listed in *Massachusetts Soldiers and Sailors of the Revolutionary War*.[11] Cutter believes several of the listings are for my fifth great-grandfather and that Elijah had multiple periods of service, while Mary insists that only one of those listed is "our Elijah." She maintains that faulty genealogical and historical research by family members and others led to misinformation being published, and she has compiled credible research data to back up her claim. This includes the apparently erroneous reference to the 4th Suffolk County Regiment etched on Elijah's gravestone.

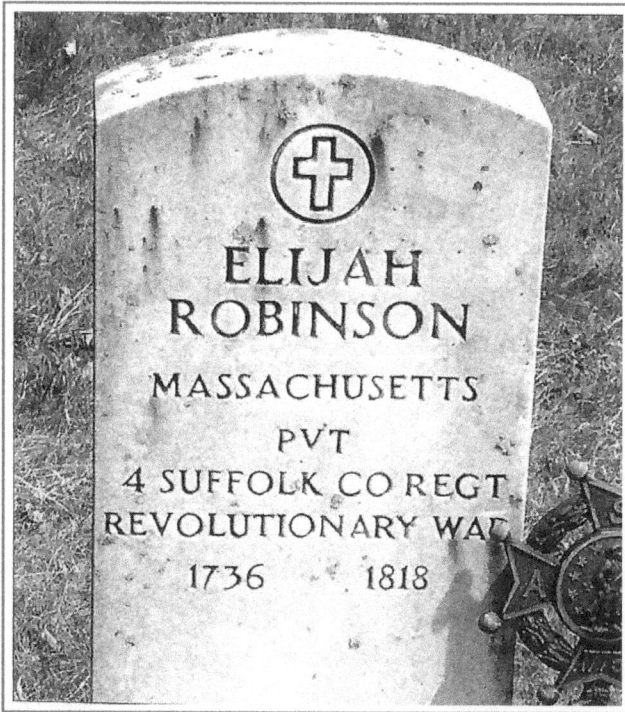

Elijah Robinson's tombstone at Fairview Cemetery, Paris, Maine.
Courtesy of www.findagrave.com.

Mary's investigation offers compelling evidence of who is not "our Elijah" among those listed in *Massachusetts Soldiers and Sailors*, and the authenticity of her research is undeniable. However, as there is no mention of participation in the Lexington Alarm among any of the Elijah/Elisha Robinsons listed in the *Soldiers and Sailors* publication, a sliver of uncertainty remains, leaving a mystery for future generations of family genealogists to investigate.

There is little doubt that "our Elijah" had proximity and opportunity to be at Lexington and Concord on April 19, 1775. Both towns were less than fifty miles from Elijah's home in Barre—forty-four and thirty-eight miles away, respectively. Word of a looming strike by the 700 British Regulars anchored in Boston's harbor was common knowledge—even before Paul Revere's midnight ride through the countryside west of Boston.

Other than proximity and opportunity, I could not discover additional evidence to substantiate historian Cutter's claim, but I have not found any evidence to disprove his assertion either. Nonetheless, both Parsons and Carter agree that Elijah's final (or only, as the case may be) period of service was from August 9 through November 21, 1781.

One hundred and thirty-four years later, in 1915, Elijah's great-grandson, Elisha Morse Stevens, applied to the *Sons of the American Revolution*. In his application, he wrote that Elijah served in Captain Jonathan Sibley's company, Colonel Luke Drury's regiment, and that he "served 3 mos. [and] 23 days . . .," then returning to his ". . . residence [in] Barre," about forty-four miles west of Lexington where it all began.

An additional layer of circumstantial intrigue adds to the mystery of Elijah's possible Lexington Alarm participation.

Numerous references from *Massachusetts Soldiers and Sailors* show that Elijah's commanding officer during his last service period was the same Luke Drury who led a group of militia, or Minute Men, who "marched on the alarm of April 19, 1775." Was "our Elijah" among them?

Regardless of the speculation surrounding Elijah's participation, he and his wife Sarah left Massachusetts sometime after the Revolution and moved to Paris, Maine. Before computers easily accessed old documents and records, Mary Parsons and her anthropologist husband Jeff uncovered the ledger of a Paris, Maine, shopkeeper and farmer named Seth Morse. They made Xerox copies of all 360 pages of the aged document, and Mary shared several pages of it with me. It shows that Elijah enjoyed an occasional drink and was a frequent visitor at Morse's store, and that he made fourteen separate purchases of alcohol between June 15 and September 30, 1807.

Elijah's drink of choice was rum, especially New England rum that he bought by the pint—presumably for take-out consumption. He also purchased libations by the glass or mug, known as "slings" and "grogs." These concoctions were a blend of water and sugar (and maybe a sprinkle of nutmeg or a twist of lime) mixed with West Indian rum. He likely consumed these potions on the premises, possibly at a counter in the store. It was "a time when actual money seldom changed hands," said Mary Parsons. "He repaid what he owed by several days of labor on Seth Morse's farm in May of 1808."

Elijah's wife, Sarah, also frequented the Morse store to purchase silk and other yard goods and food. The old ledger reveals that on October 20, 1807, Sarah purchased "a Scain of Silk" and one and a half pounds of sugar.

In her email to me on March 7, 2022, Parsons recounted this nugget of Elijah Robinson lore:

According to family oral history, as a young man he also served in the French and Indian War with General Braddock in 1755–56 and supposedly helped carry the mortally wounded Braddock off the battlefield, telling a grandson many years later that Braddock was shot by his own troops. But reliable records from the French and Indian War are hard to find, so I could not verify this.

Not much else is known about Elijah, except that he survived the Revolution and died in 1818 at age eighty-two. His gravestone rests at Fairview Cemetery in Paris, Maine, though Parsons says Elijah's body is not under the memorial marker. The stone was put up in 1926 by her husband's great-aunt, Annie I. Parsons. A letter revealed that Aunt Annie "had always been told that he was buried in that cemetery." Rest in peace, Elijah, wherever you are.

With the skirmishes at Lexington and Concord, the die was cast for war with America's mother country, and there was no turning back for the rebellious colonists.

On the home front, the Ruth family and other Pennsylvania Dutch farmers back in Berks County did their part to sustain the war effort. Says writer Katelyn Miller: "Their bountiful farms helped to supply Washington's Army during the Revolutionary War, while their sons fought for independence. The Pennsylvania Dutch comprised 25 percent of the forces fielded by Pennsylvania and ultimately 12 percent of Washington's total forces."[12]

The year was now 1777, two years after the opening volleys of the Revolution were fired at Lexington. Yet the outcome of America's pursuit of freedom from the tyranny of British rule was a crapshoot at best.

Always underfunded and short on the military armaments necessary to wage war, General George Washington and his Continental Army were often on the run.

Successes at Trenton and Princeton kept the fledgling republic's hope for victory alive, but could they realistically have a chance to prevail in a war against the most powerful adversary on the planet? Accomplishing that daunting task would require the help of a formidable ally.

Washington desperately needed a decisive victory to boost the morale of his soldiers and rally support from American colonists up and down the east coast from Georgia to New Hampshire. He also needed to convince a stingy Congress to continue to adequately fund the war effort. But, most of all, Washington and his Continental Army needed an alliance with a powerful foreign partner who hated the British as much as the Americans did—and the convincing victory at Saratoga on October 7, 1777, gave Washington all that and more.

France was still reeling from its stinging defeat by the British on the same North American soil during the French and Indian War some fourteen years earlier. Finally convinced that Washington and the colonials had a chance to prevail, France was eager to enlist in the fight and joined the Patriot cause.

Another fifth great-grandfather, Major Elijah Hyde, was attached to the Continental Army under General Horatio Gates and commanded the 2nd Regiment of Connecticut Light Horse militia. Initially, Washington and his generals were skeptical of the loosely organized, volunteer state militias, including light horse detachments like Hyde's—but that opinion would change after the 1776 campaign near New York City, where the Connecticut Light Horse militia proved its battle worthiness.

Major Hyde and his cavalry regiment were up against British forces commanded by General John Burgoyne. In June of 1777, Burgoyne's strategy to defeat the colonial rebels unfolded by marching his troops south out of the Canadian province of Quebec into New York's Champlain Valley. He planned to link up there with General William Howe's forces, marching north along the Hudson River out of New York City. Another contingent, under the command of brevet Brigadier General Barry St. Leger, was headed east from Lake Ontario.

Their objective was Albany, a strategic city on the banks of the Hudson that controlled the river and the surrounding valley. With a tight grip on Albany and the Hudson River south to New York City, they hoped to isolate and cut off the rebellious New England colonies—the epicenter of the revolution. The lower colonies, they believed, with more Loyalist leanings, could be put on the back burner.

General Horatio Gates's Continental Army, encamped near Stillwater, was the only obstacle to Burgoyne's march south to Albany. Positioned fifteen miles short of Burgoyne's target, and anticipating the confrontation of these opposing forces, Washington sent troops from his army and another contingent from the New York highlands to reinforce Gates's position. He also sent his trusted and most aggressive field commander, Major General Benedict Arnold, who would later betray his loyalty to Washington and his country for money and recognition.

For reasons beyond Burgoyne's control, his three-pronged tactic and the rendezvous with Howe and St. Leger never materialized, leaving the British general and his army to fend for themselves against a more significant force of Continentals and state militias. Burgoyne's misfortune not only proved fortuitous for the Americans, it changed the tide of the Revolution and the course of world history.

Connecticut's military forces included two cavalry units: the 4th Light Horse Militia commanded by Elijah Hyde, and a Continental Army detachment under Captain Jean Louis de Vernejoux, a French mercenary. Brevet Captain Vernejoux had previously demonstrated his command skills and battle-worthiness in engagements with the British. So, when Major Hyde was tapped to lead the combined units to Stillwater, "it probably rankled Vernejoux to be subordinated to a militiaman who had only recently been promoted to the rank of major."[13] But according to family genealogist Steve Smith, Hyde was well connected, reportedly having been appointed Major by Washington himself.[14] Further, while nosing around for the service record of Hyde's brother Ebenezer, I discovered that Elijah was a member of "Washington's staff and entertained [General] Washington and [the Marquis de La] Lafayette at the Old Hyde Homestead in Norwich [Connecticut]."[15]

On September 1, 1777, the combined Hyde-Vernejoux detachments arrived near Stillwater, and by September 6th, there was a "considerable body" of Connecticut infantry as well as light horse in camp on Bemis Heights, high defensive ground that overlooked the farm of loyalist John Freeman.[16] With fortifications on the flood plain and cannon on the heights, the colonials' position dominated all movement through the river valley. Burgoyne's army was entirely dependent upon the river to haul their supplies, and the American defenses were an unavoidable and dangerous obstacle.[17]

Thirteen days later, on September 19th, Freeman's farm was the site of the first battle of Stillwater. The British held their ground in a seesaw struggle, giving them a technical victory. The price of victory was high, though. They suffered over 600 casualties, while the American losses were a fraction of that.

Back in New York City, General Henry Clinton received word of

Burgoyne's predicament. He responded immediately, sending a contingent of British troops up the Hudson to reinforce his position. Fortunately for the Americans, the Redcoats only got within seventy miles of Bemis Heights. Once aware that Clinton's reinforcements would not arrive, Burgoyne assessed his precarious position and assembled a war council of his top field commanders. A strategic retreat north to avoid the looming conflict was among the options discussed, but the notion of a retreat, strategic or otherwise, was rejected by the British general as "disgraceful." Rather than pull back, the commander decided to attack on October 7th.

Two thousand Redcoats, more than one-third of Burgoyne's army, attacked the left flank of the American lines. However, the army the British general faced was more than 12,000 men strong, and the American general knew "the invaders [were] increasingly discouraged." Gates realized "from his spies and from Burgoyne's numerous deserters" how much trouble Burgoyne was in.[18]

With the British forces routed, the outnumbered enemy suffered 1,135 casualties in both battles (in contrast to the American losses tallied at 330 killed or wounded). By October 13th, with dwindling supplies and facing an army twice as large as his, Burgoyne weighed the reality of his near-hopeless circumstances. The following day, under the cover of darkness, he retreated north. "Hampered by bad roads made worse by frigid downpours, the British retreat made only eight miles in two days to a small hamlet called Saratoga."[19]

Only three days later, on October 17, 1777, General John Burgoyne's humiliating loss to the Continental Army and various colonial militias came to an end. "Burgoyne did not simply surrender a British army, he surrendered the first British army in world history," says Eric Schnitzer in *Hallowed Ground* magazine."[20] His military career over, General John Burgoyne returned to England in disgrace.

The battles at Stillwater, New York, on September 19th at Freeman's Farm and at Bemis Heights on October 7th are often collectively called the Battle of Saratoga. Elijah Hyde was wounded at Stillwater,[21] as was Benedict Arnold, who took a bullet to his leg when his horse was shot out from under him. Although he later returned to active duty, he never fully regained the use of his wounded leg. As for Elijah, the nature of his wound is not known. Records show he was able to witness the surrender of Burgoyne ten days later, offering evidence that his wounds were not life-threatening. We further know that at least five of Elijah's brothers—Caleb, Zina, Eliphalet, Andrew, and Ebenezer—would serve in the Continental Army, Navy, or a state militia, and that all but one would survive the Revolution.

Captain Vernejoux, the indignant partner of Elijah, remained in command of his troops until October 15, 1777, after the two major battles at Stillwater but before the surrender of Burgoyne at Saratoga. General Gates reported that Vernejoux "ran away" on that day, leaving the commander to find a replacement.[22] Perhaps the festering tension between Major Hyde and Captain Vernejoux was more than mere rankling.

Before Saratoga, the battlefield worthiness of the rebellious colonists was sometimes in question, at least by British commanders—but that opinion changed on October 7th. Quoting a British officer:

> The courage and obstinacy with which the Americas fought were the astonishment of everyone, and we now became fully convinced that they are not that contemptible enemy we had hitherto imagined them, incapable of standing a regular engagement and that they would only fight behind strong and powerful works.[23]

After Saratoga helped turn the tide in America's fight for independence, a new Franco-American alliance emerged. While France had previously supplied the Patriots with various war materials—guns, cannon, and powder—the victory at Saratoga brought them all in with foot soldiers on the ground and warships on the high seas. This, in addition to loans, helped to finance America's revolution.

The alliance with America also offered the French a chance to assuage their stinging defeat at the hands of their archenemy in the French and Indian War and regain a foothold in North America. With their valuable new ally and trading partner, the French had a chance to disrupt Britain's military ambitions by diverting and diluting its resources over three separate theaters of British conflict: America, Europe, and the West Indies.

Throughout the Revolution, the town of New London, Connecticut, was a bustling colonial seaport, mostly unscathed from the surrounding conflict. Active in the West Indies trade, it sent livestock and agricultural products to the Caribbean islands in exchange for sugar, rum, and molasses eagerly sought by New England's colonists. Historian Harry Schenawolf writes that the town "had grown fat over the years from privateering and the spoils of captured merchant ships,"[24] providing essential arms and supplies in the form of plundered cargos of gunpowder, cannons, and trade goods needed to fuel the patriot war effort. Hence, New London's warehouses became storehouses for the revolutionary cause.[25]

The relative tranquility of the bustling seaport was about to end, and three of my ancestors played a role in the town's fate. Edward Baker, in an article about the burning of New London, wrote:

In late July of 1781, the British merchant ship *Hannah* was seized [by privateers] and brought to New London. . . . She was the largest prize taken during the entire war, with a cargo of West Indian goods and gunpowder whose value was estimated at 80,000 pounds sterling. The loss spurred the British to retaliate, to punish New London for its success at privateering. Who better to command this attack than Benedict Arnold, born and raised only 10 miles away, in Norwich, and anxious for a command and to demonstrate his newfound loyalty to King George III?[26]

On September 6, 1781, just six weeks before Lord Cornwallis surrendered to George Washington at Yorktown, Virginia, Benedict Arnold led a punitive strike on the defenseless town. He seemed to revel in his treasonous attack against his former countrymen—an infamous achievement not lost on the judgment of American history. It would be Britain's last victory of the Revolutionary War and seal Arnold's fate as the most hated of all traitors. Comparing Arnold to the Bible's Judas, Benjamin Franklin reportedly described his betrayal as "a miserable bargain especially when one considers the quantity of infamy he has acquired to himself and entailed to his family."

A year earlier, Arnold had bartered his loyalty to America for a sum of £6,000—about $1,317,000 in today's dollars—and an annual pension. That, and the promise of a commission as a brigadier general in the King's army, was all it took to transform a disgruntled patriot into a treacherous collaborator. Anxious to showcase his battlefield command abilities against his former compatriots, the turncoat general led a raid that "had more to do with spite than strategy,"[27] with about 1,600 British and Hessian soldiers accompanied by some local loyalist troops against a small force of patriot defenders. One of those defenders was Major Elijah Hyde's son, Colonel Zabdiel Hyde, my fourth great-grandfather.

Born in New London, Colonel Hyde was a farmer before and after the war. According to a book titled *History of Wabasha County,* published in 1884: "Zabdiel Hyde . . . commanded a regiment of militia during the defense of New London when it was burned by the British in 1781."[28] Four years later, he married Mary Lyman—two years after the Treaty of Paris officially ended the Revolution—and they reared three children: Henry, Gershom, and Maria. Later, Hyde was elected by his neighbors to represent the town of Lebanon in the state legislature. After Mary died in 1815, Zabdiel moved to Bath, Maine.

Nearly 110 years after the burning of New London, in his application to Sons of the American Revolution dated April 17, 1891, Zabdiel's great-grandson, Frederick William Hyde, wrote:

My great grandfather Col. Zabdiel Hyde (Col. State Militia Conn) was a young man 20 years of age at the time of Arnold's expedition against New London Conn. In 1782 (it was 1781) after the massacre at Fort Griswold he aided as one of the state militia in driving the English troops to their ships and was in some skirmishes at the time of the burning of New London. My father heard him tell the story when [he was] a boy and remembers three 'Queen Ann's' guineas, which as prizes were awarded him after the British left, and which he cherished . . . till his death, in Bath, [Maine], May 15, 1842.

He was two and a half weeks shy of his eightieth birthday.

Returning to the banks of the Thames River in Connecticut, the last significant military engagement in the north began to unfold. At daybreak, twenty-four British ships packed with 1,600 seasoned troops sailed into Long Island Sound and assembled at the mouth of the Thames River. Commanded by Brigadier General Benedict Arnold, they hoped to surprise the unsuspecting Americans.

Their objective was threefold: Capture Forts Trumbull and Griswold, plunder New London's stockpile of goods and naval stores, and destroy its privateer fleet. "Arnold did not get his surprise," says historian Schenawolf. At one o'clock in the morning, his ships reached the mouth of the river. Then, just after daybreak, "they were spotted by Rufus Avery, a Continental Army sentinel at Fort Griswold."[29]

Both forts were lightly garrisoned with Continental Army soldiers. For reinforcements, they depended on an alarm system to muster local militias. Firing two cannons at spaced intervals and sending riders on horseback into the countryside usually rallied the requisite local militias and Minute Men needed to defend the town. But on September 6th, that was not to be.

In his 1882 book, *The Battle of Groton Heights*, author Charles Allyn states that New London's privateers were in the habit of announcing their successes on their return to port by firing salutes from their guns. The booms of rumbling cannon fire in the harbor became so commonplace that few on this day paid it any heed. The lackluster response by the surrounding townsfolk did little to rally the forces necessary to defend the forts and town from destruction by the Brits. He goes on to say that "The enemy, about 9 o'clk, landed in two divisions of about 800 men each, one of them at Brown's farm near the lighthouse, the other at Groton point." Lt. Colonel Edmund Eyre led the Groton Point troops, consisting mostly of British Regulars—the 40th and 54th Regiments of Foot—plus a provincial regiment of New

Jersey loyalists under Cortlandt Skinner and about fifty Hessian mercenaries. His objective was Fort Griswold, about two and a half miles due north, a march that was slowed considerably by thick forest and marshy swampland.

Although Fort Griswold was a substantial fortification, Eyre found it only lightly garrisoned with Continental troops.[30] The 120 men, chiefly militia, put up a courageous defense during the forty-minute battle, but a handful of men could not defend against a superior force of 800 seasoned British soldiers.[31] Arnold's orders to Lt. Colonel Eyre "were to burn the barracks and blow up the magazine." From eyewitness accounts, the *Connecticut Gazette* reported the massacre at Fort Griswold:

> Having a number of their party killed and wounded [the defenders] found that further resistance would be in vain, and resigned the fort. Immediately on their surrender the valient Colonel Ledyard . . . and 70 other officers and men, were murdered, most of them heads of families. The enemy lost a Major Montgomery and forty-one officers and men in the attack. . . . The troops were commanded by that infamous traitor to his country, Benedict Arnold, who headed the division which proceded to the town.[32]

The *Revolutionary War Journal* gave this account, quoting Rhode Island soldier and eyewitness Joseph Wood:

> When Colonel Ledyard found that he was not able to withstand the attack upon the fort, he opened the gate to surrender. As he did so, the British commander asked, 'Who commands this fort?' Colonel Ledyard answered, 'I did, but you do now.'

And presented the British commander his sword. The British commander took the sword and thrust it through Colonel Ledyard. This I heard and saw. Upon that, Captain Allen, who was standing nearby in the act of presenting his sword to surrender, drew it back and thrust it through the British officer who had thus killed Colonel Ledyard. Captain Allen was then immediately killed by the British. This I also saw. I then leaped the walls and made my escape.[33]

The Colonials say the slaughter of the garrison at Fort Griswold was an act of revenge for the casualties inflicted, including the killing of British Major William Montgomery. The British, of course, paint a different picture of the events leading up to the massacre of the surrendering American troops. According to historian Schenawolf:

Some argue that in the heat of battle, the American flag had been shot down. This caused the British to believe that the garrison had surrendered; however, the 'wretched rebels' continued to fire, resulting in their justified slaughter.[34]

Regardless of the actual circumstances surrounding the battle, this much is certain: the American patriots who defended the fort that day were dead. The Redcoats then headed to the nearby town of Groton, setting fire to "1 school-house, 4 barns, 2 shops, 2 stores, and 12 dwelling-houses."[35]

The *Connecticut Gazette* reported that the enemy lost 220 men and about 70 deserters. They further listed 82 patriots killed or murdered defending the fort that day, including a Pequot Indian named Tom Wansuc, who was stabbed in the neck (one source indicates he may have survived),[36] and two negroes, Lambo Latham and Jordan

Freeman, both of whom were freed slaves.[37] Freeman had been Lt. Colonel William Ledyard's "man-servant," a gift he received from his father.[38] They were reportedly good friends, prompting Ledyard to give Jordan his freedom at the start of the Revolution. The *Revolutionary War Journal* credits Freeman as the patriot who killed British Major Montgomery with the thrust of his ten-foot pike as the Major mounted the fort's rampart.

Just across the river, the British treachery continued, this time personally orchestrated by Major General Benedict Arnold.

Landing near the lighthouse on the New London side of the river, Arnold led troops consisting mainly of Redcoat foot soldiers, the 38th Foot, and around fifty Hessian mercenaries. His forces also numbered a contingent of Tory loyalists, including his provincial regiment called the American Legion.

The Redcoats were about a mile from town when Arnold ordered a detachment of men to nearby Fort Trumbull. As the enemy approached the fort, the outnumbered defenders fired one volley, killing or wounding five British soldiers. According to Arnold's after-action report, the beleaguered patriots then spiked their guns and evacuated the fort, heading for the river to make their escape.[39]

At the same time, the main body of Lobster-backs advanced to the town. There, pointing his sword toward the street and its shops, Arnold reportedly said, "Soldiers, do your duty!" The King's men then proceeded to set fire to the stores on the beach, then to the dwelling-houses. All told, 65 houses containing 97 families, 31 stores, 18 shops, 20 barns, and nine public and other buildings were burned. Several ships tied up at the wharves were also left in flames.[40]

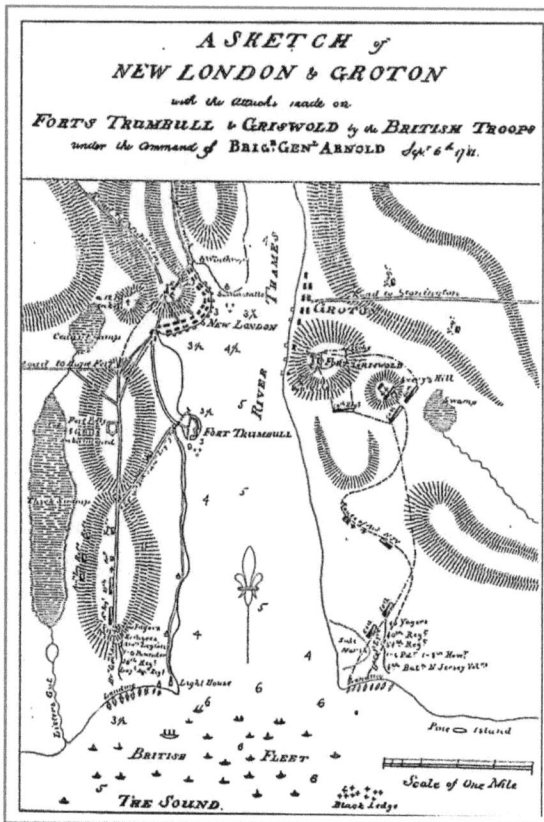

1781 British map of the Battle of Groton Heights and the burning of New London. Arnold's Battalion landed in the foreground on the left bank of the Thames, heading for New London. Eyre's troops landed on the right shore bound for Fort Griswold and Groton. Courtesy of the Library of Congress.

Two of the buildings set ablaze that day were the home and barn of Nathan Douglas, another fifth great-grandfather. He had been a farmer but sold his property thirty years prior, in 1751, to move to Bank Street in New London.[41] Thankfully, his son Ebenezer Douglas, my fourth great-grandfather, fared better with his property during the raid. His daughter, Julia, described what happened that day:

On the day New London was burned, my father, as was his practice, rose early in the morning and went out to look around, as the British were expected at any time. He soon came back in great haste, saying that the enemy were coming and he must get out his company; and that mother must take care of the three children. Anticipating such an event, they had already prepared a place of safety a few miles out of town, and taking a loaf of bread in a bag, and the youngest child in her arms, my mother started tither . . . When they returned, after the British had left, they found the house still standing but everything [else] was destroyed.[42]

Daughters of the American Revolution (DAR) records show that Ebenezer was a lieutenant in the 1st Triband (Company) attached to the 3rd Regiment of Brigadier General John Tyler. (Later records have him listed as a captain.) Not much else is known about his service during the Revolution, but after the war, he was appointed goaler (jailkeeper) and vessel inspector for the port of New London.

Eleven years later, in 1792, the state of Connecticut attempted to tally the losses. They concluded the destruction was valued at over £61,000, or about $200,000 in the Continental dollars of the day,[43] which, accounting for inflation today, would amount to nearly $13,000,000.

As for Ebenezer, he died at age fifty-one from yellow fever on September 3, 1798, and was buried at Cedar Grove Cemetery in New London.

For another Ebenezer in my ancestral line—the youngest son of my sixth great-grandfather, Elijah Hyde Senior and brother of the aforementioned Major Elijah Hyde—the Revolution caused suffering on a whole different level.

Continental naval records show that Ebenezer Hyde was a sailor aboard the *USS Confederacy,* a frigate captured on April 14, 1781, by *HMS Roebuck* and *HMS Orpheus* off the coast of Delaware. Ebenezer and his *Confederacy* shipmates were "escorted" to New York's harbor, where the ship was stripped of its stars and stripes, its flag exchanged for a Union Jack. The officers were paroled and sent home, pledging not to rejoin the rebellion, but for ordinary swabbies like Ebenezer, the treatment by their British captors was far different.

Reserving a special kind of hell for the rest of the captured sea dogs, the Redcoats sent Ebenezer and his mates to the infamous prison ship *Jersey.*[44] One of the POWs who escaped that ship was Christopher Hawkins. In his book titled *The Adventures of Christopher Hawkins,* he details the horrors inflicted on American soldiers and sailors who were captured by the Brits.

The old war boat that became the *Jersey* had been a ship of the line with a full battery of seventy-four guns and other armaments before decommissioning. During the winter of 1779–80, she was stripped of her sails and rigging and converted into a prison ship. Moored in the East river, a short distance from the Long Island shore, it held about 800 captives.

Of the many factors contributing to the horrific mortality rate on the *Jersey,* one of the most significant was the overpacked quarters below deck. "The prisoners were so crowded together," said Hawkins, "that the minimum amount of pure air necessary for the healthy functions of life was never enjoyed." Charles I. Bushnell, who authored the Introduction and Notes sections of Hawkins's book, as well as providing commentary with excerpts from letters and newspaper accounts, writes:

Another thing which added to the horror of this prison ship . . . was [the] filth . . . the [air] circulation was very limited . . . [and] the surrounding atmosphere [was] saturated with the [smell of urine and feces]. . . . The sickness seemed to be epidemic. We called [it] the blood flux or dyssentery.

Bushnell also cites two letters written home to family by *Jersey* prisoners published in the colonial newspaper *Pennsylvania Packet*. In the first, dated September 4, 1781: "I will inform you that we bury 6, 7, 8, 9, 10, and 11 men in a day; we have 200 more sick and falling sick every day. The sickness is the yellow fever, small pox, and in short, everything else that can be mentioned." The other letter was published over a year later, on January 2, 1783: "The deplorable situation I am in cannot be expressed . . . I am left here with about 700 miserable objects, eaten up with lice, and daily taking fevers, which carry them off fast."

Adding to their misery, prisoners could only answer the call of nature in the evening after dark on the upper deck. Under heavy guard, only two at a time were allowed topside to do their business. "There was no place between decks provided us to satisfy those calls," says Hawkins.

Another torment was the daily culinary experience, if you can call it that, served up by the enemy. In stark contrast to the disagreeable food served to the Ruths in 1733 onboard the *Pennsylvania Merchant*, they starved the American prisoners to force patriots into traitors. Given only one mouthful of salt pork daily, with the occasional pea soup that looked like "brown water and fifteen floating peas," the hunger was brutal. On occasions dubbed "Pudding Day" by the prisoners, the Redcoats would deliver tainted flour, rancid raisins, and raisin sticks, served in green lumps. The captives, lamented Hawkins, would pick out the sticks and mash the lumps of flour. To wash down their meal, there was the daily ration of water, always brackish and putrid.[45]

Despite the fact that this starvation strategy rarely worked to convert men to the British side, it did succeed in thinning the captive population. Each morning, prisoners were awakened to the call of "Rebels! Turn out your dead!" That cry through the open hatch into the misery below deck would muster a working party of prisoners to place the sick in bunks and carry the dead to the upper deck where they were "laid upon the gratings." A blanket was sometimes stitched around a patriot before the remains were hoisted over the side of the ship into the boat below without further ceremony.[46]

Prisoners, at least those who were able, were anxious to be chosen for the work detail. Said Captain Dring, recounted by Bushnell in Hawkins's book, "It was not so much from . . . a wish of paying respect for the remains of the dead as from the desire of once more placing their feet upon the land, if for but a few minutes."

On the sandy shore, across from their floating Bastille, they "placed the corpses on the hand-barrows, and received . . . hoes and shovels." Then, they "proceeded to the side of the bank . . . [where they] were directed to dig a trench in the sand. . . . The corpses were then laid into the trench, without ceremony; and we threw the sand over them."

Such was the manner of burial for these American patriots. Hawkins's book recounts that as they reluctantly began to retrace their steps to the boat, remains that were buried days and weeks earlier were exposed by the ebbing tide. "But at least," he adds, they "had enjoyed the pleasure of breathing, for a few moments, the [fresh] air of our native soil."

An anonymous letter, posted by Bushnell in Hawkins's book, was sent to newspaper editors in the colonies on May 18, 1783, and states:

To all Printers of Public Newspapers,

To the everlasting disgrace and infamy of the British King's commanders at New York: That during the late war, it is said, 11,644 American prisoners have suffered death by their inhuman, cruel, savage and barbarous usage on board the filthy and malignant British prison-ship, called the Jersey, lying at N.Y. Britons tremble, lest the vengeance of the Heavens fall on your isle, for the blood of these unfortunate victims!

—AN AMERICAN

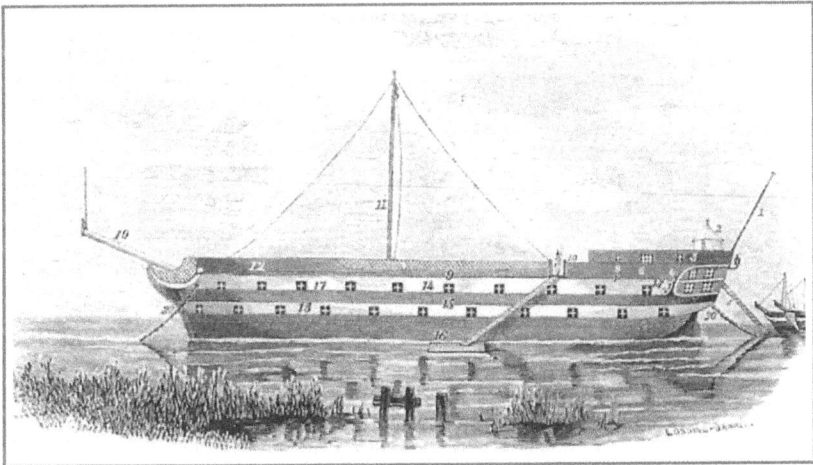

A depiction of the prison ship Jersey, moored at Wallabout Bay near Long Island, New York. The burial ground in the swampy marshland is shown in the foreground. The illustration was published without attribution in The Adventures of Christopher Hawkins printed in 1864.

On April 9, 1783, all remaining captives onboard the prison ships in New York were released, and the *Jersey* was broken up and abandoned. Most of the Ruths, Hydes, Douglases, and Robinsons returned to the families they left behind in towns and farms stretching from Pennsyl-

vania to Maine. Only one did not return to his family: after being murdered by his Redcoat captors, Ebenezer Hyde's remains are buried in
the marshy wetlands alongside a prison ship in New York's harbor,
sharing a watery grave with thousands of his compatriots—men who
chose death rather than betray their country by swearing allegiance to
King George and fighting for the Redcoats against their patriot brothers
in arms.

CHAPTER SIX

The Fledgling Republic: A House Divided

eturning to the Dutch countryside of Pennsylvania, along the Cacoosing Creek, the eight sons and several grandsons of Peter, Sophia, and Catharine Ruth came home to their bountiful farms. Once safely enveloped again in a cocoon of family and friends, they must have been filled with a renewed spirit of hope for the future. Yet, as time passed and the warm glow of victory waned, some surely must have wondered what the future held for their new nation.

While life in the former English colonies had seemingly returned to normal, the ensuing years were fraught with growing pains as the world's greatest experiment in self-governance was about to unfold. One of the most influential figures in that experiment was Benjamin Franklin.

Often referred to as the "first American," Franklin helped draft the Declaration of Independence and the Constitution—both foundational documents bearing his signature. During the Revolution, Franklin was instrumental in priming the French pump for money and arms—even before France formally joined the war effort with soldiers on the ground and warships on the high seas. And, when the colonial rebellion was finally won against the planet's greatest superpower, he was one of his new country's envoys at the signing of the Treaty of Paris. It was Franklin's signature on those papers, along with those of John Adams and John Jay, that officially ended America's long struggle with the British over control of their destiny.

Franklin knew his new country and its radical form of government were fragile from the start, and he no doubt wondered if it would be possible for free people to actually govern themselves. He and his compatriots were venturing into undiscovered territory; there was no democracy playbook to consult and only scant historical frames of reference they could look to for guidance. These former British colonists would have to chart an entirely new path—and they would have to accomplish it on the fly.

An anecdote attributed to Franklin encapsulates what many historians believe were his concerns for his fledgling country's survival. At the Continental Convention in 1787, a popular narrative notes that Franklin walked out of Independence Hall where someone reportedly shouted, "Doctor, what have we got? A republic or a monarchy?" Unflinchingly, he reportedly shouted back, "A republic, if you can keep it." His clever rejoinder portends the difficulties he anticipated for his countrymen in their quest for "life, liberty, and the pursuit of happiness."

Scarcely three generations later, Franklin's worst fears were realized.

By the mid-1800s, the industrial and agricultural states of the North found themselves pitted against the rural plantation aristocracy of the South. At stake for the Southerners was not only the continued existence of slavery in their states but its possible expansion into new states and territories. For the North, the task was to hold the Union together as "one nation under God"—one nation, that is, without slavery.

As the conflict loomed, Abraham Lincoln from Illinois was locked in a battle for a United States Senate seat. In a celebrated speech delivered in Springfield, Illinois, on June 16, 1858, Lincoln metaphorically linked his remarks to a well-known gospel verse from the Bible:

A house divided against itself cannot stand. I believe the government cannot endure permanently half slave and half free. I do not expect the Union to be dissolved—I do not expect the house to fall—but I do expect it will cease to be divided. It will become all one thing or all the other. Either the opponents of slavery will arrest the further spread of it, and place it where the public mind shall rest in the belief that it is in the course of ultimate extinction; or its advocates will push it forward till it shall become alike lawful in all the States, old as well as new— North as well as South.

Lincoln likely believed referencing words of Jesus would rouse public support for the eradication of slavery and prevent its expansion into other states and territories. But while he lost his 1858 Senate bid to Stephen A. Douglas, many historians believe his persuasive challenge to Americans—that slavery must either be "universally accepted or universally denied"—helped propel him to the White House two years later in 1860.

The shattering internal fight for the nation's soul, and for the Union's survival, rallied two separate American armies with opposing ideologies: over 2 million soldiers from the North and approximately 750,000 soldiers from the South.

In Geoffrey C. Ward's book titled *The Civil War: An Illustrated History*, the Introduction, written by Ric and Ken Burns, quotes noted Civil War historian Shelby Foote's description of the magnitude of the Civil War on the American experience:

> Any understanding of this nation has to be based . . . on an understanding of the Civil War. It defined us . . . as what we are and it opened us to being what we became, good and bad things. And it is very necessary, if you're going to understand the American character in the twentieth century, to learn about this enormous catastrophe of the nineteenth century. It was the crossroads of our being, and it was a hell of a crossroads: the suffering, the enormous tragedy of the whole thing.[1]

In their collaborative work with Ward, the Burns brothers posed these questions:

"Why did Americans kill each other? How did it happen? Who were these people who fought and killed, marched and sang, wrote home, skedaddled, deserted, died, nursed and lamented, persevered and were defeated? What was it like to be in that war? What did it do to America and Americans?"[2]

Many of these questions were answered by nine of my ancestors— all of whom served as privates in various Union infantry or cavalry regiments. Benjamin F. Washburn, my second great-granduncle, and three of his sons enlisted in the Union Army in Wisconsin. Joseph Null, my great-grandfather's brother (my great-granduncle), also enlisted, along with my second great-grandfather, John Hyde, and my great-grandfather, Levi Null. Benjamin Franklin Morse, my second great-grandmother Sarah Jane (Morse) Ruth's brother, and Benneville P. Ruth, the second great-grandson—and my third cousin, three times removed—of family patriarch Peter Ruth signed up as well.

Most of the combatants—between 75 and 80 percent—on both sides were volunteers. After the Union surrendered at Fort Sumter in mid-April of 1861, young men in the North and South eagerly enlisted. Peer pressure likely nudged some to serve the cause, while others may have simply wanted a steady paycheck and three squares a day. Most, it is believed, expected the war to only last for several weeks or maybe a couple of months at most. Some signed up for adventure or the perceived "glory" of battle, probably not wanting to miss out on the action.

These men and boys who signed up to fight had similar traits. The average recruit was a volunteer between the ages of 18 and 29. Enlistment records show four of my ancestors fell within that range—Benjamin Franklin Morse, age 19; Benneville Ruth and Levi Null, age 22; and Benjamin F. Washburn, Jr., age 24. Notably, of the other five, two were younger—Washburn brothers Frederick and George, ages 17 and 14 respectively—and three were older—Joseph Null, age 33, John Hyde, age 43, and Benjamin F. Washburn, Sr, age 48.

Most recruits had never been more than a few miles from their front porch when they enlisted, nor had they ridden the rails on a train or floated down a river in a barge. Yet more than half left their family farms to join the cause. The rest were city folks like teachers, preachers, accountants, carpenters, lawyers, merchants, painters, shoemakers, blacksmiths, and the like. Seven of my forebears listed their profession or occupation as "farmer" when they joined the military while the other two were merchants in the city. Collectively, Civil War soldiers were predominantly single, white, native-born, American men who identified religiously as Protestants.

In the final analysis, it seems most reasons for enlistment were as simple—or as complex, as the case may be—as this: the Yankee soldiers fought to preserve the Union and abolish slavery, while the Rebels fought to defend their homeland, and/or to prevent blacks from gaining an equal footing with whites. But by mid-1863, voluntary enlistments in the Union Army had begun to dwindle. To help compensate for the reduction in numbers, the federal government instituted a draft. At about the same time, they also decided to enlist Black soldiers to bolster the ranks.

The Ruths and the other Palatine pilgrims who settled in eastern Pennsylvania were peace-loving folks who had come to North America to find refuge from an oppressive and war-ravaged continent. The cultural values they brought with them to America, and the persecution from tyrants they left behind, taught them to revere liberty and personal freedom. These values extended to the issue of slavery. "Our people always protested against slavery, as they were a liberty-loving people," says Kershner and Lerch in their History of St. John's (Hain's) Reformed Church. Referring to their parishioners, they write, "Our people . . . never kept slaves, but fought against the very idea with all their might."[3] This early condemnation of human bondage carried over into the generations leading up to the Civil War.

Called the War of Northern Aggression by many Southerners, and the War Between the States by some in the North, the war that nearly tore apart the republic was also labeled the Second American Revolution, the War of the Rebellion, the Brothers' War, the War Against the States, and the War for Southern Independence. Black abolitionist Frederick Douglass dubbed it the Slaveholders' Rebellion. By any name, however, history now calls it the American Civil War.

And while Fort Sumter "was a bloodless opening" to the conflict, it turned out "to be the bloodiest war in American history."[4]

For the soldiers on the battlefield, life was brutal. Lulls in action were likely rare, and the recruits were often on picket or building breastworks—temporary fortifications. Food was frequently a challenge too: the chow served up to the battle-hardened warriors was as tough as they were. Benjamin ("Ben") Franklin Morse, my second great-grand-uncle, lamented some of the hardships in a letter to his father back home in Wisconsin, dated February 2, 1864:

> Some of their foodstuffs had to be plundered from enemy territory. The army has taken almost all the grain that was in the country to feed the army. If they had not done so, we would have to starve for the want of something to eat.

One of the staples was beef stew. The meat was cooked in big black iron pots suspended over open-flame log fires, then thickened with flour and water. The cooks would throw potatoes and any other vegetables they could forage into the concoction.[5] Most meals were washed down with plentiful quantities of coffee. Sixteen-year-old soldier Charles Nott said of the coffee: "Boiled in an open kettle, [it had] the color of a brownstone front." Nevertheless, it was often "the only warm thing we had" out in the field.[6]

Some of the soldiers dubbed their cooks "dog robbers" as a light-hearted reference to the possible source of the evening meal. Despite this, "We [would] grab our plates and cups, and wait for no second invitation," said Lawrence VanAlstyne, a soldier with the 128th New York Volunteers. "We save a piece of bread for the last, with which we wipe up everything, and then eat the dish rag."[7]

Away from camp, food was often hard to come by. "My pardner went out foraging," said Ben Morse, "and got some apples which made a very fine mess of apple sauce for me and him."[8] In fact, foraging was a way of life for foot soldiers in the Civil War—Yanks and Rebs alike. If they couldn't scavenge something from a farmer's orchard or field as they traipsed through the countryside, they could reach into their haversack for a "sheet iron cracker," otherwise known as hard tack. A durable biscuit made of water and unleavened flour, it was regularly used to ward off hunger in the field.[9]

There were also downtimes for the soldiers, when they caught up on personal items, such as washing laundry, getting a haircut, or writing letters home to family, friends, or sweethearts. Ben said, "We had our shirts on five weeks before we got a change of any clothing whatever." [10] This was, I suspect, the experience of other soldiers as well.

After their personal chores were completed, soldiers sometimes passed the time singing patriotic songs. Often accompanied by a fiddle or banjo, Yankee favorites included "When Johnny Comes Marching Home" and "Lincoln and Liberty." As for the boys in gray, "Dixie" and "The Yellow Rose of Texas" were favorites.

Other entertainment diversions included games like checkers and chess, or even baseball or snowball fights, weather permitting. And you could always find a friendly game of chance in any military encampment. Card games like poker were prevalent, along with boxing matches staged between soldiers, offering a physical outlet for their boredom. Both of these activities provided opportunities for spectators to place a friendly wager.

It is not surprising that under such circumstances, some of the men turned to liquor for distraction. Passing a jug or flask of "bark juice," as the elixir was affectionally known, or throwing back some whiskey offered jovial camaraderie for battle-hardened warriors with their fellow brothers in arms. Tapping the bottle may have also helped some seek a momentary reprieve to help deaden the memory of battles past, while others may have used the tonic to sedate the frightful thoughts of bloodshed looming in the battles to come.

Last, but certainly not least of the diversions, a contingent of camp ladies was always present to provide physical entertainment. Known as "fancy girls," these women dutifully followed the troops on horse-drawn wagons, offering "horizontal refreshments," as the soldiers called it.

All of these distractions surely helped to keep morale up during what was undoubtedly daily risk of life and limb on the battlefield. Two of my aforementioned ancestors, Benneville P. Ruth and Benjamin Franklin Morse—both called Ben—were involved in two of the bloodiest of those battles: Seven Pines, Virginia, and Kennesaw Mountain, Georgia. I've chosen to profile the lives of these family heroes—both killed in action—for two reasons: I was able to uncover a large amount of personal background information about each, including their photographs and military service records, and both of their stories offer firsthand accounts, written in graphic detail, illustrating the horror of combat.

On May 31, 1862, after a day of drenching rain on Virginia's Peninsula, the first shots echoed through the trees in the Battle of Seven Pines—also known as Fair Oaks. The clash pitted Union General George B. McClellan against Confederate General Joseph E. Johnston. The so-called "Peninsula Campaign" was McClellan's offensive up the Virginia cape bordered by the James and York Rivers. As they sat on Richmond's doorstep, McClellan's Army of the Potomac was bent on taking the Rebel's capital city. But McClellan failed and the war dragged on for almost three more years. General Johnston was wounded during this campaign and was replaced by Robert E. Lee as commander of the Confederate Army of Northern Virginia—and the rest is history.

Seventy-three thousand American troops—34,000 Union soldiers and 39,000 Rebels—amassed near the headquarters of the Confederacy. Only two days later, there were nearly 14,000 casualties involving almost 20 percent of all combatants: 11,000 men killed in action, and the rest wounded, missing, or captured. The staggering volume of human carnage over a 48-hour span produced no clear winner, yet Union General McClellan, not known to be bashful, wrote home sounding like the victor in what history now regards as a stalemate: "Victory has no charms for me," he said, "when purchased at such cost."

The official report of the 93rd Pennsylvania Regiment, dated two days after the battle, was filed by Captain J. E. Arthur, filling in for the wounded Colonel James M. McCarter. The colonel, a raging abolitionist, was a Methodist minister known for his fire-and-brimstone sermons, and his skill as an orator and influencer was not lost on Pennsylvania's Republican governor, Andrew Curtin. At his request, and with a nudge from President Lincoln's Secretary of War Simon Cameron, Reverend McCarter was asked to raise a regiment of volunteers now known as the 93rd Pennsylvania.[11]

With the evangelical zeal of a missionary, the vicar set about his task, enlisting volunteers from the community surrounding Reading.[12] A recruitment camp was set up at the fairgrounds near Lebanon. In less than a month, more than a thousand men signed up for service.

One of those recruits was Benneville P. Ruth. On October 12, 1861, at age 22, the young baptized Christian with a full beard mustered as a private in Lebanon, joining the 93rd Regiment of Pennsylvania Volunteers, Company B. He had grown up in Reading, a few miles from the Cacoosing Creek where his second great-grandfather and family patriarch, Peter Ruth, first settled 128 years before the Civil War began. State veteran records list him as a merchant by occupation, standing five foot eight inches tall, with hazel eyes, a light complexion, and sandy hair.

Photo believed to be Ben Ruth holding his rifle beside a fellow Union soldier (possibly his friend, Adam Dorn). Photo from family archives. Circa 1862.

In the battle report, Captain Arthur wrote: "On Saturday, May 31, 1862, the Ninety-third Pennsylvania left their camp at Seven Pines at 1 o'clock, P. M., to take position in the open field some 500 yards in advance of their old camp." In the ensuing battle, Colonel McCarter was critically wounded after having horses shot out from under him on two occasions.[13]

As the troops moved forward, they formed a battle line short of their target. Soon, heavy firing commenced on their right. Surrounded by woods on both sides, they could see a clearing just ahead, but getting there would prove to be a punishing task.

Moments later, the entire regiment was ordered to move to the extreme left, compelled to force their way through a thick swamp. As they emerged from the bog, but before they had a chance to form a battle line, "the enemy, who were in overwhelming force in front, opened a heavy fire," wrote Captain Arthur. "This was answered in good style."[14]

The 93rd had held their position for about an hour when they were forced to fall back a distance of thirty yards, where they again opened fire. Outflanked by skirmishers on the left, the men of the 93rd again fell back, which, according to Captain Arthur, they continued to do, fighting at each halt. Soon after, they were outflanked a second time and retreated about "150 yards to a road running through the woods. The Ninety-third formed on the road to prevent a farther advance of the enemy." Then, sometime later, "Two regiments of the enemy were seen coming toward our right at a double-quick."[15]

With attacking Rebels staged both left and right of their position, the 93rd was forced to retire to the position they first occupied. "We remained in this position for a short time," records Arthur in the report. The troops were "engaged in throwing up breast works of logs and brush . . . as a protection against the enemy's fire, whom we expected every moment to advance from the woods in front." Arthur continues: "a perfect storm of shell and bullets . . . the Ninety-third opened a heavy fire upon the [attacking] enemy . . . a force much larger than our own."[16]

Colonel McCarter's Pennsylvania volunteers maintained their position until all their ammunition was exhausted, forcing them back into a ravine.[17] Out of ammunition—with bayonets fixed on their Springfield muskets as their only defense against the Confederate onslaught—they made their final stand. "The remnant of the regiment was [later] formed in the rear of the rifle pits, where they still remain." On the run the whole afternoon and overwhelmed by superior numbers, the brave foot soldiers of the 93rd Pennsylvania Volunteers paid a heavy price for their courage in casualties, numbering 155.[18]

Somewhere amid the melee, Catherine and Benneville Ruth's second child lay mortally wounded. It is not known if Ben was shot in a hail of gunfire at the start of the battle or while fighting his way through the swamp. He could have been hit just as his soggy boots touched the dry dirt at the edge of the clearing, or he could have been struck hours later as he and his Union brothers fell back, fighting for their lives against an overpowering enemy.

According to the captain: "Many of our killed and wounded we were compelled to leave on the field, the enemy [was] pushing forward so fast and in such overwhelming numbers that we were unable to get them off [the battlefield]." At the end of his report, Captain Arthur records the names of the casualties. Benneville P. Ruth is listed among those killed in action from Company B.[19]

The day after the battle, Ben's friend Adam Dorn wrote a letter to Ben's father back in Reading, notifying him of his son's death. Adam could obviously read and write, but his spelling and grammar were unpolished, to say the least. Many of his words are spelled phonetically, with his own local twang thrown in for good measure—grammatical miscues that were common in letters from soldiers in those days.

June 1, 1862

Mr. Ruth I will rite you (a) line to let you know that we was in a Battle yesterday on Saterday near Richmond. We went in at one o'clock and fought till night. Brave [men] on the left and then the Rebels flank us on the Right and then we had to run over to the right and they came out very fast and there we fought till night very hard.

Mr. Ruth it is very hard to tell you that your son Ben is Shot in that Battel. Don't trobel your selve about it. He dide in a good caus, he fought Brave . . . only five miles away from Richmond . . . Out of our Compeny is twenty Wounded and dead . . . the Field is laying full of dead men . . .

Me and Ben is great freands together. I sed if he shold get shot I wold let his parents know about it and so I will. He diden sofer, he fell and then he diden move him self eny mor . . . I must close. Sind by his friend Adam Dorn.

Comp B 93 Regt, PV
Peck Breagade
Couch Division
Fortress Monroe, VA[20]

Five months and six days following Ben's death, muster rolls list Adam Dorn as a deserter on November 6, 1862. Perhaps thirteen months of warfare in brutal and merciless conflicts like Seven Pines had taken its toll on the brave twenty-one-year-old.

In bloody battles like Seven Pines, military archives reveal that long, deep trenches were dug to bury the dead. They fashioned "hooks made from bayonets crooked for the purpose, and all the dead were dragged and thrown pell mell into these trenches."[21] Ben Ruth was probably buried in one of those trenches on or near the battlefield, the actual site unknown, marking an ignoble end for a courageous young man serving his country.

The second oldest child in his family, Ben left behind six brothers and sisters. Nineteen years after her son's death, Ben's mother filed for a survivor's pension—presumably after her husband died—on November 28th, 1881.[22]

Two years later, in 1864, the war had been raging on for three years. Thousands of young men were dying on battlefields with little progress to show for it. People who once thought the war would be over quickly now looked at it as being an endless war, and many were beginning to believe that it was time for a compromise.[23]

The prospect of President Lincoln's re-election was doubtful, and by mid-June, Union General William Tecumseh Sherman, eager to strike a decisive blow against the rebels, seized an opportunity to attack the enemy at its heart. Known as an aggressive, battle-hardened leader with a fearsome temperament, he wanted southerners—soldier and citizen alike—to feel the pain of their decision to secede from the Union. "War is the remedy our enemies have chosen," the commander declared, "and I say let us give them all they want."

Standing in the way of Sherman's assault on Atlanta was Confederate General Joseph E. Johnston. Historian Ward states that the rebel commander's men were dug in across the face of Kennesaw Mountain just twenty miles from Atlanta. A victory here, Sherman reckoned, could destroy the southern army at one blow.[24]

One of the troops under Sherman's command was teenager Benjamin Franklin Morse. Ben was the brother of my second great-grandmother, Sarah Jane (Morse) Ruth, making him my second great-granduncle. (Family patriarch, Peter Ruth, was his second great-grandfather.) At age nineteen, according to his muster and enlistment records, he stood nearly six feet tall with brown hair and a light complexion. His clean-shaven face—except for maybe a mustache—revealed piercing gray eyes. At two or three inches taller than most recruits, he must have cut an imposing figure standing at attention in his dress blues.

Ben Morse in his uniform, from the archives of family genealogist,
Esther Ruth Smith. Circa 1864.

Ben had left his father's home in Lake County, Wisconsin, to volunteer to serve his country. A private in Company I, 42nd Illinois Infantry, he mustered on February 16, 1864, at Stone Mills, Tennessee, signing up for a three-year enlistment.[25] Like all volunteers, he stepped forward, willing to sacrifice all his tomorrows to fight for Mister Lincoln's dream of a united America, free from the scourge of slavery.

The discovery of Ben's diary opens a tiny window into the world of Civil War combat as experienced by an ordinary foot soldier—a private on the front line. The first entry in the small notebook was dated November 24, 1863, when he left Bridgeport, Alabama, to go to Chattanooga, Tennessee.[26] As Ben departed Alabama, the Union army was in the midst of a decisive battle to free Chattanooga from a two-month-long siege. Lifting the siege opened the way for the start of General Sherman's campaign to invade Georgia and capture Atlanta.

Ben burned through a lot of shoe leather over the next three months, logging some 400-plus miles on foot, marching east to Knoxville and beyond into the upper eastern part of Tennessee. There were also excursions west, back to Bridgeport, Alabama, and then back to his home base in Chattanooga.

On February 21, 1864, he wrote in his diary that he left Chattanooga for home. His regiment was placed on furlough until April 1st of that year, as the army saw no reason to warehouse soldiers for five weeks at the Chattanooga railhead, needlessly depleting valuable war material, supplies, and food before the spring offensive.

After eight days riding the rails north, Ben pulled into the Chicago train station on February 29th. A week or so later, he boarded a train bound for home in Wisconsin. On March 11th, he arrived at his father's house in Jefferson, Wisconsin, then headed south during the last week or so in March to Long Grove, Illinois, home of his sister Sarah and other family members.

In a letter to his father dated April 15, 1864, Ben recalls that visit home:

I had a good time while I was at Sarah's for they all treated me like a child and when I left every body was crying which did make it rather hard for me to leave them. . . . It was a great deal harder to leave home this time than it was before . . . I never want to see home [again] until I can see it for good.

On April 1st, Ben reported for duty back in Chicago, linking up at Camp Frye with his unit. Four days later, he and his comrades boarded a train and headed south to Nashville—and back to the war.

Train travel for Ben and other enlisted men in the army was hardly a luxurious experience. According to veteran Leander Stillwell, there were no lavish Pullman sleeper coaches with fancy dining cars while riding the rails as a Union soldier:

Such a thing as even ordinary passenger coaches for the use of the enlisted men was never heard of. . . . The cars that we rode in were the box or freight cars in use in those days. Among them were cattle cars, flat or platform cars, and in general every other kind of freight car that could be procured. We would fill the box cars, and . . . clamber upon the roofs . . . and avail ourselves of every foot of space. The engines used wood for fuel [and thick gray clouds would tumble out of the smoke stacks] and the big cinders would patter down on us like hail.

Yet, says Stillwell, he "and his comrades were 'awful glad' to ride the rails."[27] Despite the sufferings of train travel, it gave soldiers a welcomed respite from the drudgery of endless marches.

Six days after departing from Chicago, with several stops along the way, Ben and his companions pulled into the Nashville train station at about 5:00 a.m. on April 11th. It would be the last time he would travel by rail.

It took more than two weeks to march from Nashville to Chattanooga, and Ben arrived in Chattanooga just in time for the launch of

Sherman's Atlanta campaign. It would take four months of battles and skirmishes for Union troops to capture the city. Unfortunately, Ben Morse didn't live to see that day.

The rest of Ben's war was on foot, hoofing it as an infantryman trudging down dusty dirt country roads or on turnpikes, such as they were back in the day. They often trekked in pouring rain and slogged through ankle-deep mud, traipsing across streams and over rivers on pontoon bridges. Sometimes their duty included rounding up enemy stragglers, including rebel prisoners and deserters. On other days they hacked down trees with hand axes or stomped their shovels into the hard dirt, fabricating breastworks.

And then, of course, there was the inevitable warfare: the frightening brutality and violence of raw, physical combat. On those days, skirmishes were ignited from behind makeshift fortifications, or full-scale frontal attacks ensued that often included charging across open fields under withering enemy musket and cannon fire.

During Ben's enlistment, he jotted notes in his pocket diary almost every day. Some of his entries were only a couple of words or a sentence or two. But on other days, when there was more to tell, he would write more. The following are selected passages from his notebook from the last six weeks of his life.

May 9th

Just day light. All is quiet. About half past four they commenced firing and directly afterwords they brought two pieces of artillery. [An hour and a half later they] commenced firing with . . . about five shots out of the cannon. About seven o'clock we were relieved from [the] picket [line] and fell in

and marched to the front. We have a pretty good
line [as] our troops drove the rebels back from
their position about one mile.

Later that day he recorded:

About sun down, [the] 3rd Kentucky Regt. made
a charge on the rebel fort and was repulsed and
fell back to their old place.

He carefully noted in his journal the names of several senior officers who were killed or wounded during the day's assault. Later, as darkness settled over the battlefield, he jotted:

This night we laid on what they call army
feathers made out of stone as big as your head.

May 27th
Last night there was firing what kept up all
night. This morning about daylight very heavy
skirmishing commenced. . . . Heavy cannonading was
kept up until nine o'clock a.m.

Later that day, following another round of heavy artillery fire, Ben was slightly wounded when "a bullet hit me in the instep which gave considerable pain."

May 29th

The rebels commenced a heavy firing on us, but we commenced returning the shots about as fast as they could repeat them. . . . Just a little after dark we were relieved by the 22nd Regt. Ill. Vol. when we moved to the rear and got our supper and went to bed. We weren't in bed but a little while when we were routed out with a heavy fire in front. We got up and done up our things as quickly as we knew how and got into line as quickly as possible.

All through June, it was more of the same for Ben and his band of brothers in blue—almost daily combat in one form or another.

June 7th

We got orders this morning to wash our clothes for there is no prospect of moving today.

June 15th

We advanced about a half a mile further, then we found rebels enough to play with for a little while. We drove them out of their rifle pits and drove them into their main line of breastworks. We got about within 100 yards from their breastworks.

After the Rebs opened fire with artillery, the Yanks fell back several hundred yards and were later relieved. He noted:

Our loss was one killed and 5 wounded.

June 24th

This is my birthday. I am 20 years of age this day. There has been some firing on the skirmish line all day and all night.

June 25th

This morning there is some firing on the skirmish line. About 11 o'clock we got orders to clean up camp. There was some prospect of staying 3 or 4 days. So we cleaned up camp and then about 8 o'clock P.M. we got orders to go and relieve the 65th Ohio and support the pickets which were within 10 rods (55 yards) of the rebel pickets.

June 26th

There has been more or less firing on the skirmish line all night long. About six o'clock this morning there was one of Co. G. men's wounded by a stray bullet. His name was Barans.

On June 27th, there was no black ink scrawled across the page in Ben's diary. Historian Ward wrote that on that day, 13,000 Union men stormed the Confederates on Kennesaw Mountain, and failed.[28] Confederate infantry soldier, Private Sam Watkins of Company H, 1st Tennessee, described the bloody battle in his book titled, *Co. Aytch*, published seventeen years after the war ended:

It seemed that the arch-angel of Death stood and looked on with outstretched wings. . . . My pen is unable to describe the scene of carnage and death that ensued in the next two hours. Column after column of Federal soldiers were crowded upon that line . . . but no sooner would a regiment mount our [breast]works than they were shot down. . . . Yet still the Yankees came.

The hot blood of our dead and wounded spurting on us, the blinding smoke and stifling atmosphere filling our eyes and mouths, and the awful concussion causing the blood to gush out of our noses and ears, and above all, the roar of battle, made it a perfect pandemonium. . . . Every man in our regiment killed . . . from twenty to one hundred [Yankees] each. All that was necessary [to kill them] was to load and shoot.[29]

Battle of Kennesaw Mountain, Georgia, June 27, 1864. *Stand at the Angle* by Justin Murphy, 2011. Oil on canvas. Used with permission.

Three days after Ben's death, his superior officer, Sergeant J.S. Hedges, posted a letter to Ben's father, James Morse. With daily telegraph reports from the front coming across the wires, Mr. Morse was probably keenly aware that his son's unit was in the thick of fighting near Kennesaw Mountain, and he likely opened the letter from Sergeant Hedges with some measure of foreboding, hoping against hope.[30]

The second sentence written by the sergeant delivered the crushing blow: "It is with great sorrow that I have to inform you that your son Benjamin F. Morse was killed during the charge." He explained how Ben was firing his weapon as he stormed the Rebel battlements, and how he was sitting on the ground loading his gun when a bullet coming in from the right entered the back of his knapsack near the centre and passed through his body, killing him instantly.[31]

The day before writing, under a flag of truce, Hedges sent two men out to the field to bury the company's dead, including Ben and his friend Elijah Nash. "They were buried close together," wrote the sergeant, "with their blankets wrapt around them in a soldiers grave. . . . A head board was put up at his grave, with his name, Co. and Reg't upon it."

The sergeant went on to say that he deeply sympathized with Ben's father and his family, and that the company's tears were mingled with the family's in their sorrow. Sergeant Hedges ended his letter by saying, "Ben has given his life for his country, a noble sacrifice. How we hope this cruel war will soon be over before many more lives are sacrificed." He then added: "I will send you a pocket diary that Ben kept with a letter and photograph that he had rec'd from a friend."

Less than a week later, Union flanking maneuvers forced Confederate General Johnston to fall back, abandoning Kennesaw Mountain. In a month, the Union Army laid siege to Atlanta—and within two months, Atlanta fell. The success of General Sherman's Atlanta campaign virtually guaranteed President Abraham Lincoln's re-election and an eventual victory in America's agonizing civil war.

Of the four Washburn family members who volunteered for the war—Benjamin, Frederick, Benjamin Sr., and George—the latter two never came home. Benjamin Senior died in Arkansas on February 25, 1863. Sketchy records show he had been wounded in action two months earlier, but the probable cause of his death was sickness—likely diarrhea. His youngest son George perished three months earlier in a Union hospital in Memphis, Tennessee. The fourteen-year-old must have lied about his age when he enlisted.

Joseph Null, my great-grandfather's brother and my great-granduncle, received a medical furlough and died at home from an unknown sickness or disease contracted during his service to the Union. My second great-grandfather, John Hyde, was medically discharged after suffering a paralyzing stroke following a three-day, ninety-mile forced march. He remained disabled until his death twenty-four years after the war ended.

Only my great-grandfather, Levi Null, and the young Washburn brothers, Frederick and Benjamin, survived the Civil War seemingly unscathed, at least physically. The toll it took on their mental health is unknown.

"Americans slaughtered one another wholesale," wrote the Burns brothers. "Right here in America, in their own cornfields and peach orchards, along familiar roads and by waters with old American names." The authors buttress the magnitude of the human carnage saying, "In two days at Shiloh . . . more American men fell than in all previous American wars combined. At Cold Harbor, some 7,000 Americans fell in [just] twenty minutes."[32]

In all, an estimated 750,000 soldiers died fighting for their cause—more than two percent of the entire country's population. Black combatants wearing the blue were about ten percent of the army, or around 180,000 soldiers. About a third of all combatants—including nearly twenty percent of Black soldiers—were killed at the hands of other Americans, in bloody battles that resulted in staggering daily casualty counts. Most, however, died off the battlefields from sickness or disease. The vast majority of warriors, about 80 percent in both armies, were infantry. The remaining troops were in cavalry or artillery units.

The following is an excerpt from a letter President Lincoln signed to a Mrs. Bixby who reportedly lost five sons in the war. Many believe that Lincoln's personal secretary, John Hay, actually authored the words in the letter signed by the president. Regardless of the author, the eloquence of these consoling words, reprinted widely in newspapers, would undoubtedly bring some measure of comfort to thousands of parents who lost sons in the war.

> I pray that our Heavenly Father may assuage the anguish of your bereavement, and leave you only the cherished memory of the loved and lost and the solemn pride that must be yours to have laid so costly a sacrifice upon the altar of freedom.

Unfortunately, this would not be the last costly sacrifice upon the altar of freedom for several branches of our family tree.

CHAPTER SEVEN

Westward Ho:
To the Heartland

wo and a half decades before the Civil War left America devastated with hundreds of thousands of lives lost, family patriarch Peter Ruth's grandson, George Ruth—my third great-grandfather—set out with his wife Hannah and their eight children for America's western frontier.

Twenty-year-old George had married eighteen-year-old Hannah Margaretha Rose on March 4, 1810. The young couple set up their household in Berks County near Reading, not too far from Peter Ruth's family homestead in Sinking Spring where George became a farmer. But by 1828, George was feeling the wanderlust of his grandfather Peter, and the family packed up their belongings and headed to Northumberland County, northwest of Reading nearly sixty miles as the crow flies.

While family records do not reveal how the Ruths journeyed from Reading to Sunbury, they undoubtedly traveled overland on the Centre Turnpike in a horse- or ox-drawn Conestoga wagon. Depending on weather and road conditions, wagons in those days could usually cover eight to twenty miles per day—moving at a pace of about two miles per hour—with overnight stops at local taverns. According to Northumberland County Historical Society documents, at least six roadhouses dotted the pike between the two cities. Each tavern welcomed customers with brightly colored, hand-carved wooden signs perched over the front door. Whether the Ruths stayed the night in one of these establishments or camped outside by their wagon in the lot beside the inn, it's safe to assume the Ruths probably partook in some food and drink selections on the tavern's bill of fare.

Image from a 1961 Christmas card sent to relatives by family archivist Ester Ruth Smith. Etching of George and Hannah Ruth, circa 1810.

Early American life was greatly influenced by taverns; they were not merely filling stations for road-weary travelers needing food, drink, and lodging but rather the epicenter of community life for the small towns that lined the trail. In addition to being transit terminals, taverns were the central meeting place where locals could hear the day's news, interact socially with neighbors, transact business, and engage in political discussions. The only newspaper in some communities was likely kept at the local tavern, where it was delivered from the stagecoach that stopped at its door.[1]

Some taverns had fancy parlors, mostly for affluent ladies and gentlemen traveling by stagecoach. But all roadside establishments had one thing in common—a taproom. Often the largest room in the house, each bar featured an imposing stone fireplace. During fall and winter, roaring fires kept patrons warm, kindling conversation and good cheer over rum or some other intoxicating concoction. The teamsters who drove the Conestoga wagons filled with goods to stock the shelves of local mercantiles could often be seen spread out on blankets or fur robes in a semi-circle on the floor with feet to the fire.[2] Other frequent travelers included judges, lawyers, witnesses, and sheriffs—anyone with business related to the nearby court.

Sleeping rooms upstairs usually had two or three double beds, where four who were strangers to each other often slept in each other's company.[3] If the Ruth family—being a brood of ten—booked a stay at one of these roadhouses, they would have had their own room. That being the case, George, Hannah, three teenagers, four preteens between four and eleven, and an infant would have been crammed into two or three beds, with several probably sleeping on the floor.

Whether the Ruths rode in the wagon the entire time or walked beside it during legs of the journey, a leisurely trip that would take less than two hours today was a demanding five- to six-day expedition up the Centre Turnpike. Completed around 1814, the turnpike followed the Schuylkill River north past Port Clinton to Molino, then elbowed northwest to Pottsville and on through Fountain Springs, Mt. Carmel, Natalie, Bear Gap, and Paxinos. The last leg of the turnpike, about twelve miles, led to Sunbury.

A village formerly called Shamokin by the Indians,[4] Sunbury was nestled just below a fork on the eastern bank of the Susquehanna River and inhabited by about 1,000 settlers.[5] Though small, it was a bustling town. As a major center of commerce and a strategic transportation artery on the Susquehanna River, it was not only a destination but also a launching point for pioneers heading into the wilds of America's western frontier. Sunbury was also the site of regular sessions of the Pennsylvania Supreme Court, adding to its significance as a key regional hub.

After arriving in Northumberland County, the Ruths traded the rigors of farm life for a new venture in the hospitality business. According to family historian Margaret Ruth Eddy, they ran a tavern for about seven years.[6] However, my historical plunge into the Ruth family's travels to Northumberland County in 1828 differs slightly from the 1983 family reunion records regarding George's move to Sunbury. A publication of the Northumberland County Historical Society states that there is record of an inn at Snufftown (Paxinos) in 1830 under the proprietorship of George Ruth.[7] With that as a reference, it seems that George's establishment was probably not on the Susquehanna River in Sunbury as previously thought. His inn at Snufftown probably sat along the Shamokin Creek, a stream that flows into the Susquehanna River.

Validating my speculation is this: The 1830 census for Sunbury has no listing for George Ruth. But just down the road about twelve miles east, Shamokin Township's 1830 census lists George and his family as residents. (Shamokin Township is not to be confused with the town of Shamokin farther south.) Church records in nearby Ralpho Township show that George and Hannah took communion at St. Peter's Lutheran and Reformed Church in 1835. (Paxinos, Snufftown, and the townships of Ralpho and Shamokin, are all within about two and a half miles of one another.)

While in Shamokin, George's wife Hannah hand-stitched a colorful patchwork quilt, a coverlet that became a family heirloom. One hundred and one years later, my grandfather, Carl D. Ruth, visited his aunt Valeria Ruth in Owatonna, Minnesota. Recalling his 1935 visit in a letter to his cousin, Eliza Stowell, Carl wrote: "For two nights I slept under my great-grandmother Hannah Rose Ruth's handmade quilt. . . . Stitched-in was the "year of [its] making, 1834."

Whether the Ruths were enthralled by tales overheard at their saloon by the Shamokin Creek or simply felt the magnetic tug of yonder lands, in 1836 they once again decided to pull up stakes. Now with eleven children, George and Hannah joined the Westward migration."[8]

In the mid-1830s, the way west for America's pioneers was a labyrinth of rivers, canals, and Indian and military trails, plus a network of private, state, and US government roads. Many private and state thoroughfares were toll roads, often called turnpikes. Railroad construction was booming up and down America's east coast, but few passenger rail lines were active in the northwestern corridor below the Great Lakes, the direction the Ruths were headed. The three states they traveled through—Virginia, Ohio, and Indiana—only had fifty-nine miles of railroad track combined.[9] Just like their 1828 passage to Northumberland County, rail travel was an unlikely option as they headed to the western frontier.

Instead, the Ruths would have probably made their pilgrimage via the National Road, the first highway built entirely with federal funds.[10] (Although the road was authorized by Congress in 1806, construction did not begin until five years later, in 1811.) The massive road-building project kicked off in the western Maryland town of Cumberland, just south of the Pennsylvania state line. By 1818, the twenty-foot-wide road stretched to the Ohio River in Wheeling, Virginia (now West Virginia).

Unlike the earthen roads prevalent then, the engineering specifications for the National Road included the latest highway-building technology. The road surface was graded with a thick coating of gravel and dirt, covering layers of larger stones packed twelve to eighteen inches deep. Luckily, the United States government did not need to acquire the land by eminent domain for the sixty-six-foot-wide right of way; even though it cut across prairies, pastures, and family farms, property owners welcomed the road, keenly aware that easier access, and the commerce that followed, would bring prosperity.[11]

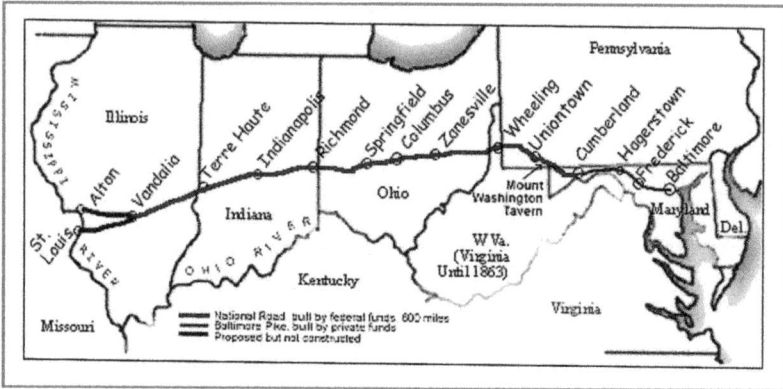

The National Road cuts a path through Maryland, Pennsylvania, West Virginia, Ohio, Indiana, and Illinois. Map courtesy of the National Park Service.

Often teeming with travelers—much like what we see during today's rush hour—the National Road was a busy thoroughfare. Crowding the road in both directions were teamsters hauling dry goods, rum barrels, coffee, sugar, and farm fresh produce in Conestoga wagons driven by six-horse teams,[12] stagecoaches filled with passengers, pony express riders and mail carriages, pedestrians, and farmers herding hordes of pigs and cattle to market.

The bustling highway also brimmed with settlers like the Ruths, driving horse- or ox-drawn wagons loaded with household belongings and supplies for the arduous journey west, often trailed by the family's cow leashed to the back end of the carriage. Traffic permitting, stage-coaches could move along the road at high speeds, often covering sixty to seventy miles per day, while Conestoga wagons, the tractor-trailer trucks of that era, averaged about fifteen miles a day.

Like today's interstate highways, the National Road offered rest stops with a full complement of conveniences at taverns spaced about every mile.[13] Two types dotted the highway: for discriminating travelers, stagecoach taverns provided fine, expensive accommodations, while more frugal travelers pulled over at wagon-stand taverns that offered accommodations for everyone else. But all taverns, regardless of class, furnished food, drink, and lodging. Plus, to accommodate the needs of horses and wagons, many of these roadside pit stops supplied livery stables and blacksmith shops.

The Fairview Inn at milestone 3 on the National Road near Baltimore, Maryland. Watercolor by Thomas Coke Ruckle. Courtesy, Maryland Center for History and Culture.

From Cumberland, Maryland, the road pushed westward through Uniontown, Pennsylvania. At Wheeling, Virginia, it branched west into Ohio past Zanesville, Columbus, and Springfield, then finally reached Indiana in 1829.[14] Entering the state at Richmond, the road pressed on through Indianapolis and Terre Haute, eventually extending its reach across the entire state by 1834. Building the road through Illinois was the last leg of the project. From end to end, the colossal multi-state construction project covered nearly 800 miles.

Like the Ruth family's earlier journey to Sunbury, no family records or documents indicate how they made the months-long passage from Pennsylvania to Lake County, Illinois; only speculation is available as to the route they traveled. My guess is they loaded their wagon, horses, and belongings on a boat or barge at Sunbury, then floated downstream on the Susquehanna River some fifty miles to Harrisburg. From there, they likely headed west overland on foot about twenty-three miles to Carlisle, picking up Forbes Road. Assuming they hiked alongside their covered wagon, children in tow, George and Hannah would have trudged for 150 miles to Pittsburgh. (Today, the Pennsylvania Turnpike and Route 30 cover most of the same ground as the old Forbes Road.)

From Pittsburgh, the Ruths likely trekked southwest some fifty miles to Wheeling. There, they would have linked up with the National Road. Their journey on America's first highway continued for about 290 miles—all the way to Indianapolis. They probably reached Indy's old Michigan Road (in Indiana), then headed north for 130 miles to South Bend. From there, they would have traversed a labyrinth of winding roads heading west, passing under Lake Michigan. Finally, after an arduous 900-plus-mile journey, the Ruth family settled on the 12th of June, 1836, in what is now Lake County, Illinois.[15]

Regardless of the exact route the Ruth family traveled to their new home, one thing is sure: George and Hannah's two-month-plus pilgrimage, herding eleven children and maybe some cows, alongside a horse-drawn wagon packed with their belongings, was an extraordinary pioneering achievement by any measure.

Arriving only three years after the first white settlers, the Ruths were among the early pioneers in Lake County. "Securing wild, unoccupied Government land,[16] the Ruth family's settlement was four miles from any post office, at what was then and is now the town of Half Day."[17] The tiny hamlet, seven miles inland from Lake Michigan and about thirty miles northwest of Chicago (some six hours away from the Windy City by horse or stagecoach), established Lake County's first post office and school shortly after their arrival. By 1840, four years after the Ruths' settlement, the population in Lake County grew from a handful of pioneers to 2,634 residents. A decade later, in 1850, the county swelled to over five times that number with 14,226 inhabitants.[18] (Today, it has over 700,000.)

With the *Land Act of 1820,* the United States Congress encouraged settlers to move west and occupy vast acres of public domain lands on America's frontier. The incentive for these hearty pioneers was large swaths of virgin territory at cut-rate prices—$1.25 per acre, a bargain even in those days. However, the government was unwilling to finance the land grab, requiring full payment at the time of purchase and registration to acquire the property.[19] For those who could afford to pay cash, the Land Act helped to create a new age of Western growth and influence. Unfortunately, it also served to further diminish territory once inhabited by Native Americans.[20]

Within two years of their arrival at Half Day, George and Hannah moved to nearby Long Grove, where they established permanent Illinois roots. US General Land Office records dated March 10, 1843, show that George purchased 162.2 acres of public land in Lake County under the 1820 Act,[21] owning the property on all four corners of the only intersection in the tiny town.[22] At $1.25 per acre, he bought the entire property for $202.75. Today's dollars would amount to $47.20 per acre, or $7,655.84, for the entire Ruth family homestead in Long Grove. The official land document bears the signatures of John Tyler, the tenth President of the United States, and Tyler's son Robert. It is likely that the younger Tyler, who served as his father's private secretary, signed both names.[23]

As in previous generations, George and Hannah Ruth were charter members of their church. Also in the tradition of the Peter Ruth family, they donated the land for the church and cemetery.[24] Just as George's uncle Christian had done in Sinking Spring, the Long Grove Church bore the stamp of generosity of another generation of Ruths.[25]

In June of 1847, George Ruth became Long Grove's postmaster. He died only three years later at age sixty-one, twelve years before his grandson George's death.

The youngest of their daughter Elizabeth's sons, George W. Washburn had volunteered to serve in the Union Army along with two of his brothers during the Civil War. He was the only one of George and Hannah's grandchildren who didn't return from the battlefield. Young George died in a Union hospital in Memphis, Tennessee, on May 13, 1862. They said it was congestive fever that killed him, though today's diagnosis would probably label it malaria. As a private in Company F, Wisconsin 2nd Cavalry, the fourteen-year-old must have lied about his age when he enlisted. He died one month and twenty-two days before his fifteenth birthday.[26]

Hannah lived another twenty years after the death of her husband, passing away in 1870, four days after her seventy-ninth birthday. The couple is buried side by side in the cemetery next to the church they helped found—now called the Long Grove Community Church.[27]

The next branch of my family tree introduces my second great-grandfather, William Ruth. One of George and Hannah's sons, he came west with his parents to Long Grove when he was six.[28] Born in Sunbury, Pennsylvania, on August 29, 1829, he "grew to manhood in the county . . . living at home [on the family farm] until he was married . . . [on] Oct. 27, 1853."[29] His eighteen-year-old bride, Sarah Jane Morse, came to Illinois with her parents from Niagara County, New York, in 1844, when she was nine. Land records reveal that the Morse family owned acreage adjacent to the Ruth property in Long Grove.

William and Sarah Jane (Morse) Ruth around the time of their marriage in 1853.

After his marriage to Sarah, William spent many years as a farmer in Lake County.[30] Then, in the early summer of 1863, records show that he registered for the Civil War draft. He was never called up, however, presumably because being the father of ten children was enough to disqualify him from service. Sarah's brother, Benjamin Franklin Morse, was not so lucky. As recounted in Chapter Six, he was killed in action at the Battle of Kennesaw Mountain, Georgia, in 1864.

Nine years later, William heeded the call of yonder lands. In the fall of 1873, he sold his farm and moved to Lancaster Township, some eighty-five miles west in Stephenson County.[31] The book, *Portrait and Biographical Album of Stephenson County, Illinois*, contains biographical sketches of prominent citizens of the county. The *Album* reports that Mr. and Mrs. Ruth settled in section eight of the town's northwestern quadrant where they were members of the Reformed Church. It also records that William was active in community affairs, serving as township tax collector and in other local offices. The last line of the sketch proudly declares, "In politics he is a Prohibitionist."

After seventeen years in Lancaster Township, with a steady influx of eastern settlers pouring into Stephenson County, the Ruths probably needed a little more "elbow room." Sparked by the wanderlust of his forefathers, William once again decided to pull up stakes, this time moving to Minnesota.[32] Census records from June 29, 1895, show they planted roots in Mantorville, a small town in southern Minnesota about 200 miles northwest of Lancaster Township. The census data lists William as sixty-five and Sarah as sixty.

Since their days in the Palatine region of Germany—long before family patriarch Peter Ruth arrived in America—the Ruth family held deeply religious beliefs. It was no different for William and Sarah. They joined the Congregational Church of Mantorville soon after their arrival, where William became an officer of the church and one of its deacons.[33]

In addition to William's involvement in the community's religious affairs, he was politically active. His position on the "devil's brew" did not change when he moved to Mantorville. As an alcohol abstainer, he ran for judge of the probate court on the Prohibition ticket in

1890.[34] But according to a township historical website, Mantorville was dealing with the alcohol issue twenty-five years before the Ruths arrived in Minnesota.[35] In 1875, an application for the town's first saloon license was up for consideration. It was soundly defeated by a vote of 138 to 118. The year before, the Woman's Christian Temperance Union —the largest women's organization in the United States—was founded in Ohio, and a branch with ten founding members was organized in Mantorville on January 23, 1880.[36] Monthly meetings were held in members' homes and at the Methodist Episcopal Church in town. By 1884, nine years after denying its first liquor license, Mantorville issued two saloon licenses. This time, the margin of victory was only one vote.

By the time the 1900 census rolled around, William recorded his occupation as a "retired farmer." Three years after that, at age 74, he died in Mantorville on October 10, 1903, just seventeen days before his fiftieth wedding anniversary. His obituary appeared on the front page of *The Mantorville Express.* Cutting through the flowery language saturating the notice, one sentence seemed to capture his personality: "In the church he was a humble, willing, enthusiastic, and spiritual worker, and as a citizen he always stood for temperance, freedom and the rights of the people."[37]

By 1919, America finally yielded to the unrelenting pressure of the temperance movement that had swept the country, and the states ratified the Eighteenth Amendment to the United States Constitution. Nationwide alcohol prohibition had begun. William surely would have celebrated its passage, though it would be repealed by the Twenty-First Amendment a mere fourteen years later.

Sixteen years after the death of her husband, on the morning of February 14, 1920, Sarah passed away. The next day, *The Daily People's Press* reported her death in its Sunday morning edition, saying, "Mrs. Sarah Jane Ruth, 84 years old, died Saturday morning at the home of her daughter [in Owatonna]." She was a "great-grandmother to four-teen children and grandmother to thirty-five."[38] William and Sarah are buried at Evergreen Cemetery in Mantorville, Minnesota.

Yet another adventurous spirit in the family line is William and Sarah's eldest son, Reuben Eugene Ruth—my great-grandfather. Though ac-counts of his early years are hard to come by, we know that he was born on September 27, 1855, while his parents were still in Long Grove, Illinois, and that he was known as "Gene" to family and friends. In 1872, when he was only seventeen, he left the family homestead in Long Grove to head northwest. Traversing nearly 300 miles, the teenager passed through Wisconsin, crossed the Mississippi River into Minnesota, and then trekked on to the small town of Mazeppa.

In those days, Mazeppa was a flour-milling center powered by a twenty-six-foot-high wooden dam on the Zumbro River.[39] It was there that Gene met a young woman named Minnesota S. Hyde. Known as Minnie, she was born in Mazeppa on February 26, 1859, the ninth of eleven children.[40] Nine years after moving to Mazeppa, the *Lake City Leader* reported that Gene married twenty-two-year-old Minnie Hyde at the home of her parents on February 17, 1881. (Other sources show the wedding day as the 26th.)

One of the pioneers who founded the town in 1855 was Minnie's father, John E. Hyde. That same year he started construction of his family home—a log cabin at the corner of First (Main) and Walnut streets.[41] Despite being a disabled Civil War veteran, Hyde was active in community affairs, and in 1866 was appointed the town's first postmaster. In downtown Mazeppa, such as it was in those early days, the enterprising Hyde also opened a mercantile business, selling yard goods and furniture. The energetic Hyde also had other firsts in the burgeoning town: On Sundays, one of his properties was used for church services, while on weekdays, it became a schoolhouse to educate Mazeppa's children.

In May of 1888, Gene once again rekindled the nomadic spirit of his father and grandfather before him and packed up his family for a move farther west.[42] This time, the Ruths headed more than 300 miles into the Dakota Territory. It is unclear what means of transportation Gene and Minnie used to make their journey; during the late 1880s, railroad lines spiderwebbed across Minnesota and into what is now eastern South Dakota, so the family could have traveled by rail. It's more likely, however, that they went by horse and wagon, using existing roads of the day. Whatever their means of travel, they landed in the small town of Kimball, where they homesteaded a tree farm.[43] Some six months later, on November 2, 1889, South Dakota was admitted as the fortieth state in the Union.

After only six years in Kimball, the Ruths backtracked forty-seven miles east to the burgeoning city of Mitchell, South Dakota, a junction for several rail lines heading north, south, east, and west, as well as the intersection of the road network, both dirt and paved. A larger community with over 3,000 people, Mitchell offered more opportunities for the Ruths' growing family. It was also more strategically located for Gene's job as a traveling salesman.

Educating their children was always high on the Ruth family's priority list. Minnie had attended the State Teachers College in Winona and taught school in Minneapolis for some years before her marriage. According to genealogist Eddy, with Gene often on the road for his job, "it was left to my grandmother to manage the family and see to it that her six children were well educated."[44] One of the benefits of moving to Mitchell was access to higher education. Dakota University, later renamed Dakota Wesleyan University, was right in town. The older children, including my grandfather Carl, attended.

"One of my favorite family stories," recounts Eddy, "illustrates the high regard for education in my father's family. After sending the first child, Marjorie, to Oberlin College it was agreed among the next five boys that none of them would get married until they had finished college and earned enough to send $1,000 back home for the education of the next brother."[45]

Gene and Minnie Ruth clan in front of the family home in Mitchell, SD. (L to R) Standing: Chester (Chet) and Edgar (Ted). Seated: Cora (Carl's wife), Minnie, Marjorie, Rena (Ted's wife), Gene holding Dean (Ted's son). Front: Charles Webber (Marjorie's husband) holding daughter Ruth, George, and Carl with son Robert (my father). Missing from the picture is son Irwin. Photo circa 1914.

Much of what I learned about Gene's life was gleaned from obituary notices published in multiple newspapers. Stuffed in file folders packed with family records, these clippings opened a tiny window into his life and death. Regrettably, the names of the publications had been cut out of the clips; most of the rest came from family reunion records and notes scribbled on slips of paper.

For twenty years, Gene earned a living on the road as one of the early salesmen of canned goods for a Minneapolis firm, spending days away from home visiting outlying districts.[46] One of the unidentified newspaper accounts suggests he was blessed with the gift of gab because "he was well known over central and southern South Dakota." In those days, men who hit the road selling their wares were called "commercial travelers." Today's vernacular might more aptly call them "traveling salesmen" or "road warriors."

Providing for his family's well-being was a priority for Gene. He was an active member of United Commercial Travelers, a fraternal society providing a host of welfare benefits for traveling salesman and their families. Like his forefathers, he was a man of faith and planted Christian roots in Mitchell. One of the unidentified newspaper articles said, "He was one of the best church workers in the city and was a senior deacon at the Congregational Church."

Toward the end of his career, probably tiring of the long days on the road away from home and Minnie, Gene made a job change. One of the unknown newspaper accounts stated that for the past three years he had been in the real estate and insurance business in Mitchell.

One of the mysterious clips about Gene uncovered in the family files reported that he and Minnie left Mitchell on an extended trip (presumably in late fall of 1916). Around the turn of the century, a new mode of transportation revolutionized how Americans traveled from place to place. With the introduction of Henry Ford's mass-produced Model T in 1908, auto ownership and tourism surged. While there is no mention in family records regarding their mode of transportation, the Ruths planned an eastern excursion to visit their children over several months. My guess is that this road warrior planned to drive his automobile the whole way.

Roads, paved and unpaved in those days, were a patchwork assortment of arteries stretching across the United States. Some roads were marked with identifying signage, but most were not. According to a 1915 Rand McNally road map called *Auto Trails Map of the United States,* one of the paved thoroughfares was the Lincoln Highway. Limited to automobile traffic only, Lincoln opened for business in the fall of 1913. It was the first transcontinental highway in the United States, stretching from New York City to San Francisco.

Surely, an experienced commercial traveler like Gene would have stashed a copy of the *Official Automobile Blue Book* in his glove box. The *Blue Book,* a navigational aid and travel guide, was essential equipment for any motorist venturing farther than their memory could take them. The book was packed with city maps, service station locations for gas and repairs, hotel and hospital names and locations, and road-by-road and turn-by-turn directions for numerous marked and unmarked urban and rural roadways.

A typical entry in the *Blue Book* read like this:

SIOUX FALLS, 10th St. & Phillips Ave. Go north with the trolly on Phillips Ave. [At] 7th St.; turn left 1 block and then right at the Court House on Maine Ave. . . . Caution for sharp left turn just beyond. Curve left past state penitentiary. . . . Follow [telephone] poles straight north.

The directions continued like this until travelers reached their destination. The *Blue Book* was the early twentieth century's version of today's *Google Maps* or a car's built-in GPS navigational system.

Assuming my hunch is correct, Gene and Minnie would have

headed southeast in their automobile from their home in Mitchell, motoring some seventy-five miles to Sioux Falls. Depending on road and weather conditions, the Ruths' cruising speed probably varied from fifteen to maybe thirty miles per hour. If they averaged twenty-five miles in an hour, arriving at their daughter Marjorie's home in Sioux Falls would have taken about three hours. I'm not sure how long they stayed in Sioux Falls, but after they visited with their daughter and her husband, Charles Webber, they packed up and hit the trail again, this time for Cincinnati, Ohio.

With South Dakota at their back, the Ruths likely zig-zagged the roads southeast to Davenport, Iowa. It is a 342-mile beeline, but on the tangled network of paved and unpaved roads of the day, their tires probably rolled fifty to 100 miles farther. They would pick up the Lincoln Highway in Davenport, pointing their auto due east for 284 miles. On the open road, with the "pedal to the metal," Gene could easily average twenty-five miles per hour. At that speed, the Ruths could rack up 150 miles of daylight motoring in a six-hour day. (Without streetlamps to illuminate the way, driving in those early days was restricted to daylight hours.)

The Lincoln Highway looped south around Chicago and under Lake Michigan. When they reached Fort Wayne, Indiana, Gene and Minnie probably turned straight south on another road for the last stretch to Cincinnati. The final leg likely took them about six more hours and covered about 140 miles.

Regardless of the actual route, the couple's travels from Sioux Falls would have surely taken them through the center of America's heartland, crossing three states before reaching Cincinnati, the home of their sons Edgar and George. Newspaper clips show that Edgar was a professor of engineering at the University of Cincinnati and that his younger brother George was a student in the engineering school. Later that same year,

George and two of his older brothers would be fighting for their lives in the trenches of France, against foes from the motherland of their third great-grandfather, Peter Ruth.

After the reunion with their sons in Cincinnati, Gene chauffeured Minnie northeast to their next port of call—Cleveland, on the shores of Lake Erie. After two days on the road, logging about 250 miles on the odometer, they pulled into town. Their son Chester—"Chet" as he was called—worked as a reporter for a local newspaper, the *Cleveland Leader*.

Sometime after their arrival, Gene took ill. One of the anonymous newspapers, quoting from a story that appeared in the *Leader*, said that "R. E. Ruth . . . died suddenly last night at Lakeside hospital after a short illness. Pneumonia developed from a slight cold a week ago and was the cause of death." The date was February 15, 1917. The obituary, possibly written by Chet, said that Reuben Eugene Ruth was sixty-one years old and that arrangements were made to ship the body to Owatonna, Minnesota. Funeral services were scheduled to be held at his mother Sarah's home, "and thence, to Mantorville [Minnesota], his old home for burial." It further described that the deceased was one of the pioneer grocery salesmen in this locality, covering much of South Dakota for a period of 20 years.

Had Gene lived, he and Minnie would have probably traveled another 300 miles to Washington, D.C., to visit their son Carl, his wife Cora, and their grandson Robert—my dad. At the time, Carl was a journalist working in Washington as a correspondent for the *Cleveland Leader* and several other newspapers. If Gene and Minnie had completed their months-long tour, the round trip would have covered over 2,500 miles.

After Gene's death, Minnie moved to Sioux Falls to live with her daughter, Marjorie Webber. A trailblazing mother who reared six children—often alone—while her husband was on the road, Minnie ensured her offspring all had an opportunity to attend college, and five of the six did. Her five sons served in World War I, three of them battling the Germans in France. Two were wounded in action and received Purple Hearts. All of her children had successful careers and raised families of their own.

The young pioneer woman Gene married in 1881 back in Mazeppa, Minnesota, lived another eighteen years after her husband's death, passing away on October 6, 1935. The headline of her obituary—garnered from a clipping I found from an unidentified South Dakota newspaper—declared, "PIONEER DAKOTAN CALLED BY DEATH, Mrs. Minnie Ruth . . . Succumbs After Brief Illness."

In a letter to his cousin Eliza, my grandfather Carl wrote this about his mother:

> Her death had brought us all together in the same place for the first time in thirty years – and more. And we all silently thanked God for such a glorious Mother. We had seen her hands calloused and bleeding many times in those early Dakota years and each one of us had given her pain. . . . She had a marvelous buoyancy and cheerfulness which carried her triumphantly over all the suffering and adversity. And her simple faith that all was for the best and that somehow God in His goodness would take care of us all, was sublime. I would rather have the memory of such a mother than millions in material wealth.

Minnie's obituary in the *Mantorville Express* noted she was a member of the Sioux Falls chapter of the Daughters of the American Revolution.[47] She certainly had little difficulty qualifying for membership: she came from thoroughbred American stock going back to the 1630s. As profiled earlier in this book, her great-grandfather, Zabdiel Hyde, fought in the Revolution, as did his father, Major Elijah Hyde, and five of his brothers. One of the major's siblings, Ebenezer, died at the hands of the British on the infamous prison ship *Jersey* in New York City's harbor.

While Gene's parents, William and Sarah Ruth, were still in Illinois, a teenager named Christian Walker was coming ashore at Ellis Island, New York. In a family history album that my father, Robert, assembled several years before his death in 2000, he wrote:

> In the mid-1860s, war clouds were gathering as Prussia pre-
> pared to fight Denmark and then Austria. . . . Many youths,
> especially in the southern part of Germany, headed for Amer-
> ica to avoid the rigors of service in [Chancellor Otto von]
> Bismarck's army. Young Christian [Walker, my grandmother
> Cora's father] was one [of those youths].

Boxes full of old letters, photographs, and other family memora-bilia stuffed every nook and cranny of Dad's retirement home in Boca Raton, Florida. With the tenacity of a White House reporter—albeit a retired one—he embarked on a mission to bring order to chaotic family records. He assembled a set of five family history albums titled *The Ruths*. Every page was crammed with family photographs, each with identifying captions or short narrative descriptions about family life and the times in which they lived. Some pages contained colorfully illustrated maps drawn by Dad, while others were photocopies of newspaper front pages highlighting momentous world events.

The narrative from one of those albums profiled his grandfather,

Christian Walker. Christian came to America when he was seventeen with about twenty other villagers from Kirchentellinsfurt, Germany. Like most of his traveling companions, Christian was confirmed in the Lutheran faith. He and the others set sail from the European continent in November or December of 1866, making the voyage across the Atlantic Ocean on the French steamship *William Penn*. The trip took two weeks and three days. Within only weeks of landing at Ellis Island, New York, Christian boarded a train and headed west.

At noon on January 1, 1867, Christian disembarked from a Rock Island Railroad coach in Ottawa, Illinois, a small town southwest of Chicago. Sometime later, he settled in Ransom, about twenty miles southeast of Ottawa. In the old country, he had been a carpenter but in America, he bought some real estate—enough land to take up a new trade as a farmer.

After moving to Ransom, he met a local girl named Margaretha Geheber, also known as Margaret, or Maggie. Her parents, both native Germans, had settled in La Salle County, Illinois, before Maggie was born. Christian married their twenty-one-year-old daughter in Ransom on April 7, 1877, some ten years after he first arrived in Illinois. During the ensuing years, he and Maggie raised seven children. One of them was my grandmother Cora.

Before her father died in 1933, Cora jotted down handwritten notes about her father. They were recovered from an old steamer trunk of my dad's and are stored in Christian's Ancestry.com file. "Father's money that he used to come here [to America]," said Cora, "was about $200." The sum was "borrowed from his father with the promise of a return as soon as [he] earned [enough to repay the debt] or else [it was to be] taken out of his [inheritance from his father's] estate." Christian paid off the debt in two years working for several of his uncles, then struck out on his own at age twenty-five.

"With father's handiness with tools," wrote Cora, he "had more work than he could do – Hiring 3 or 4 men under him to help and he got all the work he could do and more. [It] was right after the Civil War and carpentering work was more than plentiful . . . building [homes, barns,] churches, school houses, and everything that came along. Sometimes doing farming along with it." Cora further noted that during this time, many people were coming west, some in covered wagons. Railroads were being built everywhere, little towns were shooting up, and "everybody was busy."

Walker family portrait, 1895. (Left to Right) Standing: Mary-Marie, Philip, and Cora. Seated: Lester, Christian, Pauline, Margaret (Maggie), and baby Ella.

Heeding the call of this westward expansion—fifteen years after setting foot in Illinois and five years after his marriage—Christian gathered his family and left Illinois behind for Cook Township, 410 miles farther west and eight and a half miles south of Schaller, Iowa.

According to title records uncovered by his grandson Elwood C. (Woody) Walker, Christian purchased 312 acres of open prairie on November 22, 1882, paying just $6,600—$21.15 per acre. The title records show Christian's down payment was $1,700 and that he financed the remaining debt with two mortgages of $2,900 and $2,000. A *Des Moines Register* article published on December 12, 2021, lists farm prices in the vicinity of the Walker property topping out at $11,987 per acre. Based on this valuation, the Walker homestead would be worth just over $3.7 million today.

Under a portrait of the Walker family in one of the Ruth history albums, my father described life on the Walker farm in Schaller:

> In summer the sun beat down remorselessly on humans, animals, and crops. Storms were frequent and of frightening intensity. In winter the blizzards were so blinding that guide ropes [were strung] from house to barn to keep the Walkers from getting lost. In the heavy snows, wagons were replaced by sleds which Christian built.
>
> Christian also built a house and barn, put up fences, acquired horses to pull plows and cattle to fatten on abundant Iowa corn. In the German tradition, he worked hard, conserved his resources, and soon had made the farm a profitable enterprise.

Sadly, Christian's wife Maggie died on a Wednesday evening in 1925, "aged 69 years, 7 months, and 8 days" on the 16th day of September. The cause listed on the death certificate was breast cancer. A newspaper clipping from an unknown paper wrote that funeral services were held Saturday afternoon at 2:30 at the family home on Main Street in Schaller. The article noted that Christian and Maggie had previously moved to a house in town in the spring of 1902 and had retired from farm activities. The service was officiated by her pastor, the Reverend B. M. Watson, where she was a long-time member of the Methodist church.

Christian led a long and productive life, surviving Maggie by eight years. His death notice in *The Schaller Herald,* dated Thursday, November 2, 1933, described his passing: "Slowly the weaknesses of old age waged war against his rugged constitution until the end came on the evening of October 28, 1933, when he passed away at the age of eighty-three years."[48]

While Carl Ruth—one of Gene and Minnie's five sons—was growing up in Mitchell, South Dakota, an energetic young farm girl some 216 miles away in Schaller, Iowa, was earning money to further her music education. Under the watchful eye of Cora Marguerite Walker—one of Christian and Maggie's daughters—her brothers were instructed to hoist the family's upright piano into the back of a buckboard. With her precious keyboard secured, Cora climbed aboard. According to family lore, she steered her horse-drawn wagon down dusty country roads, rambling from one farm to the next, giving piano lessons to neighboring farm children.

With the wages she earned, she attended the Sac Institute in Sac City, Iowa—about fifteen miles east of the Walker farm—where she graduated with a degree in music. Later, she enrolled at the Conservatory at Oberlin College in Oberlin, Ohio, during the 1905–06 school year. Oberlin had been the first college in America to open its doors to women back in 1833, and it was here that Cora met the man who would become her husband—my grandfather, Carl D. Ruth.

In January of 2023, I emailed Oberlin College inquiring about my grandparents, and they uncovered some interesting nuggets. One was a 1967 letter from my father, Robert, to Oberlin, asking for information about his parents. Dad wrote:

> I had often heard my father . . . and my mother . . . speak of Oberlin. Some of . . . [their] comments were quite amusing, like the way boys and girls were separated when they went to the drug store . . . for a soft drink. And to think Oberlin was way in advance of its times, even allowing boys and girls that close together.

Cora M. (Walker) Ruth as a young woman.
Photo from family archives.

This restless young woman with a passion for music possessed the same family wanderlust that many of the Ruth ancestors had. That adventurous spirit would carry her far beyond the cornfields of Iowa—traveling to places she probably never could have imagined—from America's heartland to the epicenter of world power and prestige, the nation's capital city. With her husband's influence as a prominent Washington newspaper correspondent, she and Carl were regular guests at White House receptions hosted by presidents Wilson, Harding, Coolidge, Hoover, and Roosevelt.

CHAPTER EIGHT

The World Wars: More Sacrifices on the Altar of Freedom

*B*y the beginning of the twentieth century, German-Americans and their culture had successfully assimilated into mainstream American life, and many people of German heritage had risen to positions of influence and distinction. The 1910 United States census reported that nearly nine million Americans (about nine percent of the entire US population at the time) had been either born in Germany or had German parentage—the largest, by far, of any other nationality.

The outbreak of World War I changed all of that.

As a pall of anti-German sentiment infiltrated most American communities, the warm, proud glow carried by German-Americans faded. A Library of Congress article titled "Immigration and Relocation in US History" describes it this way:

The coming of World War I brought with it a backlash against German culture in the United States. . . . German American institutions came under attack. Some discrimination was hateful, but cosmetic: The names of schools, foods, streets, and towns, were often changed. . . . Physical attacks, though rare, were more violent: German American business and homes were vandalized, and German Americans accused of being "pro-German" were tarred and feathered, and, in at least one instance, lynched.

The most pervasive damage was done, however, to German language and education. German-language newspapers were either run out of business or chose to quietly close their doors. German-language books were burned, and Americans who spoke German were threatened with violence or boycotts . . . and the centuries-old tradition of German language and literature in the United States was pushed to the margins of national life, and in many places effectively ended.[1]

While the patriotism of the Ruth family never wavered, it was against this backdrop of anti-German sentiment that our family was again called to serve.

The descendants of Peter Ruth fought and died to help save America's soul during the Civil War. Fifty-two years later, Peter's American descendants would be called to a faraway continent on the other side of an ocean—this time to help save the soul of the world. Just as they had in the Revolution and later in the Civil War, the Ruths again shed their blood, answering their country's call to arms.

Some called it "the Great War," while others simply called it "the World War." But most regarded it as the "war to end all wars." The singularity of those monikers implied that it was a unique event—the one and only—without a follow-up act. But, as we now know, the Great War was not destined to be a one-act play.

The Ruth family enclave in Lake County, Illinois, was first pioneered by George and Hannah Ruth in 1836. The ensuing years brought a flood of brothers and sisters, aunts and uncles, and a slew of cousins. Three generations later, one of those progenies was a young lawyer from Hinsdale, Illinois, named Linus C. Ruth, Jr., the third great-grandson of family patriarch Peter Ruth.

In 1914, Linus, Jr.—the son of Judge Linus C. Ruth, Sr.—graduated second in his class from Chicago's Kent College of Law. Three years later, with the prospect of a brilliant legal career ahead, the twenty-six-year-old abruptly resigned from his position at the prominent firm of Calhoun, Lyford, and Sheehan. He was probably still basking in the glow of winning his first case in the Illinois Supreme Court when, on April 6, 1917, just six days after America declared war on Germany, he volunteered for service in the 1st Illinois Regiment (later called the 131st Illinois Infantry).[2] By that time, the war in Europe had been raging for thirty-three months, and millions of people—both soldiers and civilians alike—had already perished.

Before being shipped overseas, Linus and his regiment went into training at Camp Logan, Texas.[3] Army boot camp in those days typically lasted three to four months and was administered at more than thirty sites around the country. Here, America's doughboys received instruction on the use of weapons—including rifles, bayonets, hand grenades, and machine guns—along with hand-to-hand combat, trench and gas warfare, trench construction, and close-order drilling.

Linus C. Ruth, Jr., at age 17 in 1909.
Photo from the family archives of Esther Ruth Smith.

A little over a year after America declared war, with basic training behind him, Linus and the boys of the 131st were shipped abroad as part of the 33rd Division. Their troop transport ship, the *USS Leviathan*, formerly a German luxury passenger liner, set sail for Europe on May 22, 1918, out of Hoboken, New Jersey. At the time, the *Leviathan* was one of the largest and fastest ships in the world. With a top speed of twenty-two knots, it could slice through the frosty waters of the Atlantic Ocean at nearly twice the speed of traditional troop transport ships. Unlike most other transports, it was thought to be too fast for German U-boats to catch, allowing it to cross the Atlantic without an escort.

Once they docked at the harbor in Brest, France, Linus and his mates split up for further battle training. Some were sent to train with the Brits, while the others were billeted with the Australian Corps. On July 4th, in an attack that aimed to secure the village of Hamel from German occupation, the boys from Illinois saw their first action. It was said that the Americans, totaling about 1,000 men, advanced with the Australians and promptly secured their objective.[4]

Thirty-five days later, on August 8, 1918—some seventy miles north of Paris—the Germans occupied a fortified position on high ground above the north bank of the Somme River. After a difficult night march of nearly thirty kilometers, Ruth and his 33rd Division brothers were close to the enemy stronghold. By late afternoon the next day, double-timing part of the last four miles, they reached Chipilly Ridge. At 5:30 p.m., the Americans and their British partners attacked the enemy in "one of the hottest attacks of the spring offensive."[5]

In spite of heavy machine-gun and artillery fire, Sergeant Ruth and his comrades cleaned out the German machine gun nests in the Chipilly woods and drove the hostile troops from the northern end of the Ridge.[6] But during the assault, Ruth was hit by a machine gun bullet that shattered the lower bone of his left leg. Medics evacuated him to a nearby field hospital, where he endured two surgeries. Sadly, the young lawyer from Hinsdale, Illinois, succumbed to the deadly infection that engulfed his body, forty-two days after suffering his injury.

Four months after Linus died, his best friend, Sergeant Jackson Sells, wrote a sorrowful letter to Linus's mother:

> He fell [while leading a charge] after his superior officer had been killed. . . . [Linus was] suffering intense pain . . . [as] he lay on the field of battle amid a veritable hell [storm] from artillery and machine gun fire. . . . The stretcher bearer who

carried him back received the English medal of Honor—so dangerous was the work [of his rescue].

Sells ended the letter to Mrs. Ruth by saying, "In your sorrow must be mingled a pride . . . [because your son] willingly . . . gave his life that the world might remain a decent place to live in."[7]

The obituary from an unnamed newspaper, said that "In a soldier's cemetery high on the chalk cliffs of France that overlooks the English channel is buried Hinsdale's sixth son to die in service in the present war—Linus C. Ruth."[8] In 1921, at his mother's request, Linus's remains were repatriated to American soil, and he was buried beside his father at Bronswood Cemetery, Oak Brook, Illinois. Ella, his mother, joined them there twenty-six years later.

Other Ruths followed the lead of their Illinois cousin Linus, joining America's call to arms. Among them were the "South Dakota clan"— the five sons of Reuben and Minnie Ruth—which included my grandfather, Carl, who served as an Army intelligence officer stationed in Washington, D.C. His two brothers, George and Chet, joined the Marines and fought side by side in the trenches of France. Both brothers were wounded in combat, and each received the Purple Heart. His brother Irwin, a sergeant in the Army Signal Corps, also saw action in France, while brother, Edgar, served as a captain of engineers at Ft. Sill, Oklahoma. The brothers served in a war against the same country their third great-grandfather had emigrated from 184 years earlier.

The children of Reuben and Minnie Ruth.
Left to right in order of birth: Margery, Carl, Edgar, Irwin, Chester, and George.
1935 photo from family archives.

In the fall of 1972, my dad, Robert, was in Denver, Colorado, visiting his father's brother, George Washington Ruth. Dad used the occasion to ask his seventy-six-year-old uncle about his combat experiences during World War I. Reluctantly, George—who was a corporal in the Marine Corps with the 97th Company, 6th Regiment of the 2nd Army Division—agreed to reveal some of the story. Dad, a White House reporter, interviewed his uncle using a tape recorder. Incorporating content from a transcription of that recording, along with supporting documents, George's account of the war on the front lines is offered as follows.

The war in Europe started for George and his brother Chet on October 31, 1917. More than a thousand soldiers, including the Ruth brothers and fifty nurses, sailed on the *Von Steuben* from New York, the ship's maiden voyage after converting from passenger liner to troop transport. Professor Salvatore Mercogliano in *Sea History* magazine states:

Marine Corporal George Washington Ruth, standing in uniform, holding his rifle. Circa 1917.

"The issue was not just training and equipping an army of over two million . . . but the successful transportation of this new army across the Atlantic. . . . Its pre-war force [had] numbered only 133,000."[9] He goes on to say that with America's declaration of war on the 6th of April, 1917, the army seized the ninety-one German ships that had been interned in port in American harbors. One of those vessels, the *Krownprinz Wilhelm,* later commissioned as the *USS Von Steuben,* would transport George and his Marine companions to war.

In the open Atlantic, German U-boats posed a substantial threat to these troop transport ships.[10] Because slow-moving boats, bobbing alone in the ocean, were an easy target for a sub commander, convoying proved the solution to thwarting individual attacks.[11] George told my father they were in a convoy of four ships: the *Von Steuben,* the *America,* the *Agamemnon,* and the *Mt. Vernon.* Nine days later, on November 9, 1917, naval records reported that the *Agamemnon* collided with the *Von Steuben*. The crash caused significant damage to the bows of the two ships, and both lost men overboard or had passengers who sustained injuries.[12] The website *History Central* writes that the impact was so violent that "one of *Agamemnon's* . . . soldiers fell from her deck during the collision but landed on the *Von Steuben's* forecastle and [miraculously] escaped injury."[13]

The two ships had been practicing zigzagging maneuvers, a tactic designed to make them more elusive targets for enemy submarines and their lethal torpedoes. Luckily, after the crash, both vessels were still seaworthy. Two nights later, off the French coast, this near calamity was a blessing in disguise.

At dusk, George, Chet, and several of their buddies sang songs on the top deck while sitting in one of the lifeboats. George recalled: "All of a sudden, one of us saw a smooth line coming [across the water]." They instinctively shouted, "Submarine, torpedo!" Seconds later, "the bugler sounded general quarters, and the machine guns started pumping, and there was a general alarm all over the ship."

Fortunately for the Ruth brothers and their shipboard companions, the deadly German torpedo—meant to send the lightly armed *Von Steuben* to a watery grave on the ocean floor—narrowly passed in front of its bow. George reasoned that the torpedo only missed his ship due to damage caused by its collision with the *Agamemnon* several days earlier.

The sound of an engine's turnover is how a submarine calculates a ship's speed sighted in its scope. According to George, while the turnover of the engines was normal, the *Von Steuben*, with its damaged bow, was not making the speed its engine turnover rate would typically indicate—a stroke of luck for the Americans. An accurate calculation of speed by the U-boat commander would have spelled disaster for the nearly defenseless ship.

The next day, the *Von Steuben* and the other three ships in its convoy delivered their valuable cargo of fighting men—as well as the women who tended their wounds of war—to the port at Brest, on the northwestern coast of France. George remembered that after nearly two weeks at sea, everyone was glad to reach land. From there, he, Chet, and the other Marines headed south by rail nearly 350 miles to Bordeaux—an inland city about thirty miles from France's southwestern coast. By early March of 1918, the Ruth boys from Mitchell, South Dakota, and their fellow Marines were on the move again.

Traveling over 400 miles by train, their cross-country destination this time was Chaumont, a small, central-eastern city nestled in the foothills of the Vosges Mountains. Our boys had completed their initial "boot camp" training in the States at Port Royal, South Carolina (now known as Parris Island), and now they would undergo further training at the American headquarters nearby. Ideally, the average American combat soldier had six months of training in the United States before being sent overseas.[14] Then, once they arrived in France, they received two or three months of additional training before they were deemed ready to meet the enemy. The recruits were instructed on using the latest weapons, battle strategy and tactics, and the finer points of trench warfare, along with seemingly endless drills and physical conditioning.

Once this extra training was behind them, the next stop on their combat itinerary was Dugny, not far from Verdun. George said that in most of the towns, only a few chimneys were standing among the ruins. The area was called the "quiet sector [because] the Germans were there, but it was common understanding [between combatants] that there would be no firing or raids except raids for information."

George described the battlefield, saying it was hard to imagine the trenches that existed there. Most were on hillsides and were eight-, ten-, or twelve-foot-deep. "No-man's-land was about half a mile wide," said George. One day, Ruth and a Marine buddy were led through one of the trenches by a Frenchman toward an outpost at the bottom of the hill, occasionally feeling a pistol at their backs as the Frenchman gave the countersign to indicate they could move forward.

Later that night, more American troops arrived at the quiet sector in Dugny. "The Germans knew something was up," George explained, "because they kept putting up star shells over no-man's-land," presumably to illuminate the battlefield. "That was our initiation in the front lines in a so-called quiet sector."

The stillness in Dugny didn't last long. According to George, "On the night of the 11th or 12th of April, some eight- or ten-inch naval guns blasted all night, trying to hit [enemy] ammunition dumps. On April 13th, the Germans retaliated with high explosives and mustard gas, [which] burns whenever there is moisture." As soldiers scrambled to escape the poisonous clouds, their body heat—and the sweat it generated—acted as a magnet for the deadly gas.

The German attack occurred along a five-mile front. All night long, high explosives and mustard gas shells rained down on the Americans. As the shells hit the trees, the mustard gas splashed down, severely injuring many of the soldiers. One company suffered casualties of nearly 50 percent of their men. That night, George slept with his gas mask on.

The following day, worried about Chet, George walked about a mile and a half through the woods to check on his brother. (Although they were in the same company, the brothers were in different platoons.) George said his feet never seemed to touch the ground as "the boughs of the trees were so dense because of [the] heavy shelling."

When he finally reached Chet's platoon, George learned his brother had been evacuated to one of the front-line hospitals—a casualty of the mustard gas shelling that occurred the night before. Several days later,

George himself had a delayed reaction to the mustard gas and was evacuated to one of the hospitals as well.

George recalled that the ambulance driver who took him to the hospital thought his name sounded familiar. Several days before, the driver had taken an injured Marine named Chet Ruth to a hospital that was quickly filling up with wounded soldiers. With Chet's hospital overflowing, the driver took George about fifty miles from the front to a French hospital at Pierrefitte (presumably Pierrefitte-sur-Aire). He said he felt lucky to be in a French hospital because, at that time, American doctors didn't have any experience with mustard gas, which is one of the most deadly types of gas. George remembered seeing thirty or forty mortally wounded comrades in one of the wards, dying because they were all coughing. "It was a terrible sound that I heard," he said.

While the concussion from bursting explosives was painful, they had to hit you first to do any lasting damage. This mustard gas was different, however, because it permeated through the area where it landed. George saw cases where a drop of blood oozed out every pore of a man's arm. Fortunately for George, the deadly gas had not penetrated his lungs.

After witnessing the horror other patients in his hospital were enduring due to mustard gas exposure, George decided to forgo drinking water for the next month. His only liquid consumption, during thirty days of voluntary water deprivation before being discharged from the hospital in May, was wine, coffee, and warm milk.

Chet, in the meanwhile, had already rejoined the company, mostly recovered from his wounds, and was out of the hospital. Luckily, only his eyes had been exposed to the toxic gas, which meant he was not permanently disabled. George rejoined the company a few days later, just in time to be loaded into French *camions* (trucks) heading north to Paris, up toward Flanders. He joined the 1st Division and was in one of the two regiments of Marines engaged in direct fighting as part of the 2nd Regular Army Division.

Once they looped around Paris and were heading north, the troop transports suddenly stopped. Hastily, the *camions* reversed course and backtracked on the same roads. When they reached the Paris-Metz road, the trucks headed east about twenty-five miles. At the town of Meaux, the soldiers were dropped off by the side of the road. "It was the 31st of May, I think," recalled George. It turned out that there was a good reason for the abrupt change of plans: the Germans had broken through the allied lines near Chateau Thierry a little farther along the Paris-Metz Road.

George recollected that on the next morning, June 1st, "Chet and I were scouting around and came to [an abandoned] farmhouse at a place [we] called Lucy Boo (Lucy-le-Bocage). The French had pulled out only an hour or two before." Thankfully, the Ruth brothers, like their ancestors who had fought in the Civil War before them, had learned to forage off the land. "We had to look for food, potatoes, and so forth because we just had emergency rations for three days," said George.

Foraging on the battlefield in the middle of a war often requires creativity, and the Ruth boys from Mitchell, South Dakota, were blessed with that quality in spades. The brothers nestled in a stand of trees, eating hard tack and cooking bacon in their mess kits, heated by the flames of several candles. At one point, off in the distance, they spotted a beefy, four-legged forager—a stray cow wandering across the battlefield.

Since it was technically French property, they hesitated to shoot the cow outright. Instead, they coaxed the cow over to the area where there were more cannon shots so that she would be killed by enemy fire. The evening's menu for the Ruth brothers included free-range French beef—probably with enough leftovers to feed the whole platoon.

On June 6th, exactly one year after Chet and George enlisted in Cleveland, Ohio, the Marines trekked to Bouresches, which was not far off the road near Meaux. Four days earlier, the Germans had captured the town and set up defensive positions. They also employed balloons with aerial spotters to pinpoint the source of Allied shelling. It was here that the boys were in the second wave of an attack that started out of the trees and continued across 500 yards of level ground planted in grain.

The destruction at the town of Bouresches, on the edge of Belleau Woods, where George Ruth, Chet Ruth, and the 6th Marines fought. Photo courtesy of the Library of Congress.

The Marines spread out as they cautiously traipsed through the wheat field. Their captain went out ahead of them with a German shepherd dog, the enemy bullets aimed at the Marines whistling as they flew through the stalks. (As my father recorded George's recollections, he puckered his lips and made a whistling sound simulating the deadly projectiles.) "You could see the dog biting at the bullets as they slowed down coming through the wheat," said George.

George continued: "My luck was with me right there [because just ahead of me was] Spike Shannon, an engineer from Chicago [who was shot by about seven bullets in his left leg]. I was able to get him over to the edge of the trees and call for the [medics] and then get back in position." By nightfall, they'd reached the town and started digging a trench near a building, hoping it would provide cover from the Germans' heavy shelling until morning.

The next day, the 7th of June, George caught sight of a German sniper aiming at some of their men. Wasting no time, he scrambled toward a farm building at the end of their line. Retrieving a ladder from the cellar, he climbed up into the eaves and under the clay tile roof. He directed the firepower of his Marine buddies by shouting down to alert them to where their shots were going. As a result of George's actions, they were successful in taking out the sniper.

Just as George was making his way back down the ladder, two shells blasted through the roof. The explosion knocked George unconscious, and he was taken to a sick bay in town. The next morning, he was evacuated to Meaux, about twenty miles west, where he was tagged and given morphine. He didn't have a wound on him, but some days later, still unconscious, he was transferred to Red Cross Hospital Number 5 in Paris. He was later told that he "was doing some raving." After he came to, George said he couldn't keep his head still. Three days after that, he was evacuated by rail to a casualty hospital south of Brest, on the northwestern coast, to complete his recovery from shell shock.

Sometime later, George was sent to a casualty camp the Marines had opened south of Paris along the Cher River. He was given a light duty assignment—acting police sergeant—and Chet joined him there. Chet had been hit by a piece of shrapnel through his helmet at Soissons, but fortunately, his head wound was not too severe.

With George's health finally improving, he requested to go back to the front, but his Marine doctor denied the request. Some days later, reports said the Marines would disband the casualty camp entirely. With this news, the doctor gave George the choice of going on MP duty in Paris or going back to the front with his company. George chose his company and soon reunited with his Marine brothers in the 97th.

By late August, nine or ten weeks after George's injury, both Ruth brothers were on their way to the St. Mihiel front—just in time for the major offensive. Under the command of US General John J. Pershing, the four-day battle at St. Mihiel started on the 12th of September with American Expeditionary Forces and 110,000 French troops.

The general planned a coordinated attack on a giant bulge in the German lines called a "salient"—a rough triangle jutting into Allied lines, 35 miles wide and 20 miles deep, with the small city of St. Mihiel sitting on its southwestern point.[15] In addition to ground forces, Pershing's offensive also utilized airplanes and tanks in the assault.

Unknown at the time to George and Chet, their brother, Sergeant Irwin (Ernie) Ruth, also fought in the St. Mihiel offensive with the Army's 316th Field Signal Battalion.

As George described it, the "fast action drive" by his Marines in the 2nd Division and the other allied forces "straightened out" the bulge in the German line. But there was a heavy price to pay because, according to George, "That salient was very damaging to the French and American armies. . . . I saw cannons firing point-blank at us by the Germans. We were that close to them, within maybe a thousand yards, but all you are doing is trying to get out of the line of fire if it's coming right at you." All tolled, the Allied casualties in that attack numbered over 7,000, including 2,500 killed in action.

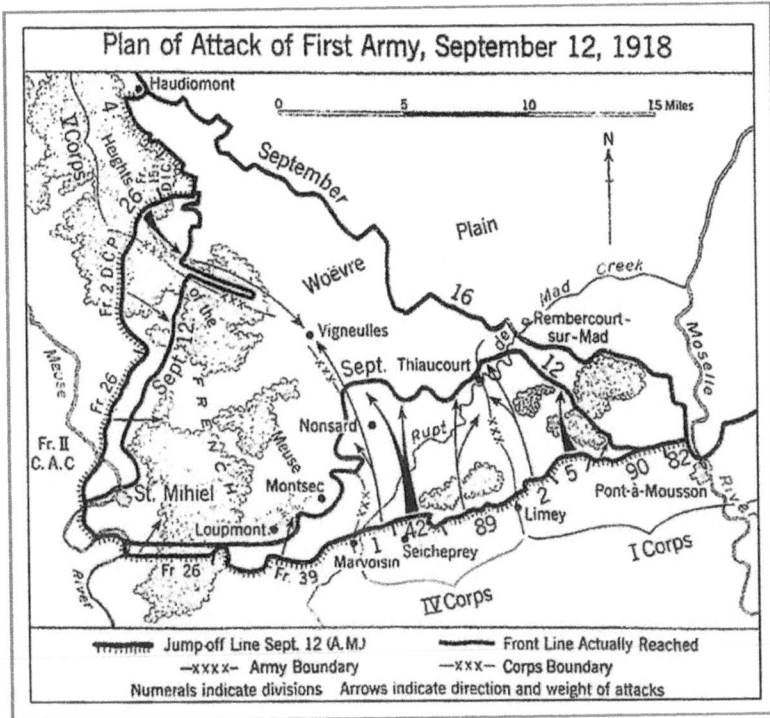

Map showing the salient (bulge) with St. Mihiel in the lower left.
Courtesy of American Battle Monuments Commission.

As always in wartime, the Marines were on the move to the next battlefield. This time, they landed nearly 250 miles south of St. Mihiel, near a village called St. Etienne. Here, George counted 180 French airplanes bombing the Germans and their ammunition dumps ahead. The French didn't get too far, however, recalls George. On the 3rd of October, when they joined the front line, "the Germans were well entrenched and had lots of pillboxes on the slopes." Many men were lost.

Fighting side by side, George and Chet were directly in the line of fire. "We got flanked," said George, "and in a clearing, we were caught by machine-gun cross fire, and several of the fellows got their legs hit. But we made our objective. [In the distance, we] could see the spire of St. Etienne out ahead. We could also see the Germans. They were about 500 yards away, but we got some of them all right."

The Marines dug a line of foxholes, but in no time, the enemy started shelling. George said that the Germans were bettering their aim each time, resulting in the near decimation of their men. Luckily, neither of the brothers was hit during the enemy bombardment, though they were left fighting with only 25 percent of their company strength.

By November, the last drive of the war had begun. Once again, the 2nd Division was given a central part of the line. Mustered on the banks of the Meuse River, rumors swirled among the troops that peace was going to be declared. On the night of the 10th, the 2nd Engineers tried to throw a pontoon bridge across the Meuse, but many were killed. Some made it to the other side, but George and the other Marines lamented the losses, believing the operation wasn't necessary.

On the next day, the 11th of November, the armistice was declared, and fighting ceased. George recalled the day as "bright and restful." Although "there were no more shells, it is hard to imagine you could relax. . . . I just remember it was a great relief that seemed to be beyond anything you could realize at the time."

At the end of the recording session that day, reflecting on his war experience, Dad's uncle George finished with this:

There's one thing about war on the front lines—it's worse to think about it when you're not there than when you are there. The noise, the thunder, the guns and all, [they] gear you up so that you are not thinking in terms of how terrible this is. You are thinking about what your job is, and you're [just] going ahead.

George was twenty-three when he returned home from the war. A year later, he was living in Cincinnati when he married Elizabeth Sidle on December 28, 1925. The couple raised two children and eventually moved to Denver, Colorado. They spent the rest of their lives in the mile-high city, where George retired as a sales engineer with the Colorado Tile Company. He died there at age seventy-seven on January 1, 1974, little more than a year after my dad recorded his wartime experiences. He is buried in the Fort Logan National Cemetery in Denver with Elizabeth.

Note: Family historian Steve Smith produced an award-winning YouTube video incorporating my father's tape-recorded interview with his uncle George Washington Ruth. In 2018, the documentary—titled *George W. Ruth, United States Marine, World War I*—won the Marine Corps Heritage Foundation's Major Norman Hatch Award. It can be viewed using the following link: https://bit.ly/George-Ruth-interview.

Also noteworthy here is that men were not the only casualties of World War I. The fifty Army nurses who sailed with the Ruth brothers on the *Von Steuben* were only a fraction of the 25,000 American women who served overseas.[16] The Army Nurse Corps alone had over 10,600 women in their ranks, not including around 300 physical therapists. Approximately seventy American women were killed during the war, according to the American Battlefield Monuments Commission. The women served as civilians, Army Nurse Corps, American Red Cross, YMCA, Army Signal Corps, and Army Medical Corps members. These heroes are buried in American cemeteries throughout France alongside their fallen warrior brothers.

Sadly, the First World War was not the end of global conflict. It was merely the prelude to another, even more destructive war.

In 1935, when my father was twenty-three, he and his friend Charlie Schmidt quit their jobs at the *Cincinnati Post* and left for Europe. They spent the summer biking around the French coast, sleeping in haystacks near Normandy, and hanging out in Paris, where they had part-time jobs with United Press International, covering for some vacationing UPI reporters.[17] While searching through a box of old family records, I uncovered a carbon copy of a five-page letter Dad wrote to his parents, Carl and Cora Ruth, back in Washington, D.C. The following selected passages from that letter describe the gathering storm.

July 22, 1935
Number 3, rue des Italiennes,
Paris, [France]

Dear Mother and Dad,
Today we are back in Paris working on the United Press staff here. Yesterday evening Charlie and I got into Paris on the rapide (train) from Strasbourg after a very pleasant journey through Germany.

Dad then outlined, in detail, his explorations and adventures in various German cities, including Heidelberg, Frankfurt, Strasbourg, Coblenz, Bonn, Coln, Hildesheim, and other historic towns along the Rhine. These cities were some of the same ones that our family patriarch, Peter Ruth, floated past on his way north up the Rhine to Rotterdam in the summer of 1733.

In the evening we arrived in Berlin and found a hotel near the
station. . . . While in Berlin we met the [United States]
ambassador and had about 15 minutes of conversation. I
obtained the impression that although Mr. [William] Dodd
admired the Germans for certain qualities, he thought they
lacked one important thing; namely the art of self-government.

A day or two later, my father and Charlie continued their tour
south to Dresden and then west to Leipzig.

On down at Weimar the next day we found out that Hitler was
in town and we waited around several hours to see him. He
finally came out of the hotel in an automobile and I got a
glimpse of him, at the same time trying to juggle my camera so
as to get a picture of him.

Boca Raton News reporter Vin Mannix describes Dad's adventure:
"Swept along by a frenzied crowd, they saw Hitler being paraded
through town in a long, open Mercedes." Then, quoting Dad, Mannix
wrote, "He was in a black uniform, so were the men in the car with
him. I was close enough," said my father, "that if I'd had a [hand]
grenade, I might've changed the course of history."

On page three of the letter to his parents, Dad described his posi-
tive and negative impressions of German life. But some of the last lines
he wrote—and the foreboding they conjured—were ominous.

The most disturbing thing about German life is its rampant
militarism. There is nothing else like it in Europe: I never saw
so many uniforms in my life, even in the small places:
Germany is building up a great, strong army and there can be

little doubt of that fact even after making a rapid trip through the country. Never did I see an officer over 25 years of age, and that means that the militarists are building for the future. And woe unto France when that day comes.

The US ambassador to Germany, William Dodd, whom my father met with briefly, was appointed by President Franklin Roosevelt in 1933. Dodd, frustrated by his inability to sway the State Department or rally the Roosevelt administration to the peril Germany posed to Europe and the Jews before the start of World War II, resigned four years later in 1937.

Four years after my father sent the letter to his parents—two years after Ambassador Dodd's resignation—Adolph Hitler's Nazi Germany invaded Poland on September 1, 1939. England and France declared war on Germany two days later, signaling the official beginning of World War II.

Two years after that, on December 7, 1941, the Japanese sneak attack on the unsuspecting US naval fleet anchored in Pearl Harbor, Hawaii, brought the Americans into the worldwide conflict.

World War II saw the extermination of upwards of seventy million people—three percent of the world's entire population. It was fought primarily on the European continent, the British Isles, North Africa, and a handful of islands scattered throughout the Pacific Ocean. Like most twentieth-century wars, the majority of victims were non-combatants—innocent civilians who were mostly women, children, and the elderly.

If there was ever a conflict throughout world history that defined what was good and what was evil, it was this one.

Fast forwarding nearly twenty years to the mid-1960s, two new branches were added to the Ruth family tree—both continuing a legacy of service to our country.

Until my brother Bob and I went to college, our limb of the family tree consisted of people with almost pure German blood. That would change when we both married our college sweethearts, fortifying our German bloodline with the addition of Irish and Italian stock.

My wife, Kathleen (Kathy) McHugh, was a Texas girl. We met at the University of Maryland and were married on August 10, 1968, in the chapel at the National Naval Medical Center in Bethesda, Maryland (now called Walter Reed National Military Medical Center). We've spent most of our fifty-five years together raising our family fewer than twenty miles from there.

My brother Bob met his wife, Katharine Cataldo, while attending Wagner College on New York's Staten Island. They were married on September 25, 1965, in New York City. Several years later, they moved west to Ohio, raising their family in Buckeye country in a small town near Columbus called Grove City. A couple of years ago, Bob's wife (who also went by "Kathy") told me her uncle, Charles J. Garibaldi, was killed in World War II when she was a small child.

Born in New York City in 1922, Charlie was the second of four children of Caesar (Babe) and Anna Garibaldi. The family lived in an apartment at 86 Thompson Street—the corner of Thompson and Spring Streets in Manhattan. During the summer of 1942, while working for the Navone Brothers Trucking Company, nineteen-year-old Charlie registered for the draft at the Washington Square draft office: Local Board Number 3.

Early the following year, Charlie enlisted in the Army. By then, he was married to his sweetheart, Rose Caccioppoli, a girl from the neighborhood. Their son, Charles Jr., was born while his dad was away at Army boot camp. While home on leave, Charlie was able to see his newborn son briefly before shipping out to the war in Europe. During that leave, he shared a premonition with his father, Babe. "Dad, I won't be back," he said. "I'm not going to make it."

A year and a half later, the twenty-one-year-old Army private's fateful foreboding was realized. While two battalions of his brothers in the 359th Infantry, 90th Division, stormed Utah Beach on D-Day, it is believed that Charlie and the rest of the 359th landed a day or two later. Almost six weeks after the Normandy invasion, he was struck by enemy fire and died of his wounds on July 18, 1944. He is buried at Calvary Cemetery in Long Island City, New York.

Private Charles J. Garibaldi. Circa 1943.

CHAPTER NINE

Arlington:
The Beautiful City
of the Dead

*O*ne of my earliest childhood recollections is being chased by my big brother, Bobby, through endless rows of glimmering white marble tombstones, the graves perfectly aligned with military precision as if choreographed by iconic World War II hero General George S. Patton himself. Three years older, my brother easily caught up to me, wrestling me to the ground. We playfully rolled in the manicured lawn between the grave markers, staining our bare knees green from the freshly mowed grass. When you're only five or six years old, the decorum of hallowed ground gives way to the youthful joy of being a child. It was the first of many Memorial Day memories of family pilgrimages to Arlington National Cemetery.

Off in the distance, the sound of our parents' shouts summoned Bobby and me back to a shady knoll on Grant Avenue. On a gently sloping hill, under a stand of tall trees, was the grave of my grandfather, Carl Ruth.

I briefly introduced Carl in the previous chapter as an Army intelligence officer stationed in Washington, D.C. But that is only a snippet of my remarkable grandfather's story.

Back in his hometown of Mitchell, South Dakota, Carl attended Dakota University (now Dakota Wesleyan University), earning a Bachelor of Science degree in 1905. Later that same year, he enrolled at Oberlin College, where he met his future wife, Cora Walker, during the 1905–06 academic year. After a year of study at the northern Ohio college, the two friends headed in separate directions: Cora to Ida Grove, Iowa, to teach music in the public schools, and Carl to Cleveland, Ohio, to start a promising career as a journalist.

Carl D. Ruth in Washington, D.C. Circa 1930.

With his formal education behind him, Carl landed on the staff of the *Cleveland Leader*. After three years of seasoning, the paper sent him as the *Leader's* bureau chief to Columbus, Ohio. Although separated by nearly 700 miles, Cora and Carl stayed in touch, kindling their budding romance. Nearly five years after leaving Oberlin, they were wed on March 9, 1911, in Franklin County, Ohio. Four years later—with my father, three-year-old Robert in tow—the *Leader* transferred Carl to the nation's capital.

In Washington, Carl's beat was politics—Congress and the White House. His profession gave him a front-row seat to "the greatest show on earth" on the world's biggest stage. During presidential election cycles, he was on the campaign trail, shadowing the White House contenders. As a passenger on the "presidential express," he accompanied the various candidates as their train excursions crisscrossed America, stopping in large cities and small towns alike. At each "whistle stop," the presidential hopefuls made stump speeches about hope and change from tiny platforms on the tail end of the last car. Eager crowds, rallied by local political organizers, swarmed the tracks surrounding the candidate. After each stopover, Carl wired dispatches back to his editors, where his stories made front-page news in hometown newspapers across America's midwest, northeast, and beyond.

Every four years, his bosses sent him to the Democrat and Republican conventions held in cities like Chicago, St. Louis, and Philadelphia. Carl's columns reported national politics from early in the primary season through the November general election. Whether writing stories from the floor of national political conventions or penning articles about the daily goings-on from the halls of Congress back in D.C., his columns kept his readers informed and up to date on the political happenings of the day.

In a March 18, 1933, letter to his cousin, Esther Ruth Smith, Carl playfully described his job as a journalist in Washington, D.C.:

[I'm] grinding out pollyticks, Congress doings, inauguration news, New Deal dope . . . from early in the morning until late at night – for newspaper readers in Newark, N.J., Columbus and Toledo, Ohio, Duluth, Minn., and elsewhere around the continent . . . in my unending search for news.

The letter's second page struck a more serious tone, expressing some of the privations brought on by the Great Depression and his hopefulness about President Franklin Roosevelt's recent election.

The inauguration was impressive. There were more people here than ever before but the financial crisis made it a very quiet and sober one. Lots of people who had been planning to come were unable to do so for lack of cash and many who did come, trusting to checks, found themselves stranded with banks closed and hotels refusing to accept their scraps of paper.

Roosevelt rose to the occasion magnificently and gives every promise of keeping up the good work. If he succeeds in pulling this country out of the quagmire of defeat and despair he will deserve unanimous reelection in 1936.

Politically, Carl was a Republican, but his letter to cousin Esther clearly showed his admiration for the recently elected Democrat president. Unlike journalists today, Carl didn't make himself part of the story. In those days, he and his colleagues in the press corps simply reported the news. It was a different era—when balance and fairness meant something. Those were the two holy commandments of journalistic ethics. Most reporters didn't have a hidden political agenda cloaked in their stories—and, even when they did, readers could barely detect the writer's political persuasion.

Carl was revered among his colleagues in the Washington press corps, the politicians he covered (and sometimes exposed), and those who read his columns in the dispatches he sent back home to their local newspapers. No one could have foreseen the news of his sudden death from Typhoid fever on January 25, 1936, and it sent shockwaves through the nation's capital city. The *Toledo Blade* reported that "Cabinet officers and members of Congress [alike] were shocked at Mr. Ruth's passing."

My grandfather's funeral was held at Washington's Church of the Covenant – First Presbyterian Church, where he and my grandmother attended Sunday services with my father as a boy—and where Carl was an active member and elder.

Four days after his death, Congressman Louis Ludlow of Indiana rose to pay tribute to his friend from the US House of Representatives floor. The following is an excerpt from the Congressional Record:

> Mr. Chairman, there are times when the tongue cannot speak the language of the heart, and that is the fix I am in today when I rise to pay my feeble but sincere tribute to . . . Carl D. Ruth, late correspondent of the *Toledo Blade* and other newspapers. . . . News of the death . . . shot like a thunderbolt through the hearts of thousands like myself whom he had befriended and it has left us staggering under an oppressive sense of loss. He was a prince among men.
>
> Snow blanketed the earth when we buried him today in the beautiful city of the dead across the Potomac . . . we shall not forget him, and we can only say with aching hearts: Good-bye old friend.[1]

My grandmother Cora—the Iowa farm girl who gave piano lessons from the back of a horse-drawn buckboard—lived independently after Carl's death in the Wardman Tower, apartment 702-G, of the Sheraton Park Hotel (now the Washington Marriott Wardman Park Hotel) in Washington, D.C. She passed away thirty years later in 1966 and is interred with her beloved husband on Grant Drive, Section 7, at Arlington National Cemetery.

Not far from the shady hillside at Arlington, where Grandfather Carl rests, was another reason for our annual pilgrimages. On the high ground up the hill, just beyond the Tomb of the Unknown Soldier, was my other grandfather's headstone. Perry Null—my mother's father—rests in the shadow of the Spanish American War Memorial, a towering metal structure with the haunting remains of one of the masts from the battleship, *USS Maine*. After a sudden explosion, the ship sank in the harbor at Havana, Cuba, on February 15, 1898. It is not known if the destruction was due to sabotage or an accident, but its sinking helped ignite America's war with Spain. Grandfather Perry was a veteran of that war, serving as a private in the Indiana Infantry.

After graduation from Genoa High School—fourteen miles southeast of Toledo in Genoa, Ohio—family records show that Perry briefly taught school. After that, he traveled to Indiana to attend Angola College for two years. According to *The Sandusky Register*, when war broke out with Spain in April 1898, the twenty-one-year-old was one of the first to volunteer, enlisting in the 157th Indiana Infantry as a private and serving in Cuba.[2] Other records reveal that the 157th was trained for battle but was held in reserve and never left the States. Regardless of where Perry served, seven months later, the war with Spain was over and in November 1898, he was honorably discharged.

After the war, Perry spent the next eight-plus years as a traveling salesman for the Arbuckle Brothers Company. They were the first roaster to package coffee in one-pound bags, making it easy for customers to purchase the caffeinated beans in small quantities. Later, he also sold packaged sugar after Arbuckle added the popular sweetener to its product line. According to notes found among my mother's papers, Perry, one of their top salesmen, was given a diamond ring and a rolltop desk by his company in appreciation for his work.

Perry left Arbuckle Brothers around 1906. On the road again, he took a job selling cash registers. Home base was his parents' farm in Genoa where he bunked down between his long-distance sales calls. About that time, Perry made the acquaintance of a young woman named Dorothy Sturzinger. Her parents, Gottlieb and Dorothea Sturzinger, both German immigrants, had settled in Perkins Township in Erie County after their marriage in 1869.

Dorothy, the youngest of the ten Sturzinger children, attended Shepardson College (now Denison University) in Granville, Ohio. Later, she transferred to Northwestern College in Naperville, Illinois, to earn her degree. After college, she returned home to Ohio as a school teacher in Perkins, just south of Sandusky. Eventually, she moved to Genoa, about forty miles west of Perkins, to teach music—as my grandmother Cora did—in the public schools.

Dorothy and Perry met at the Methodist church in Genoa, where they sang in the choir. According to my mother, Virginia, after exchanging glances for several weeks, Dorothy worked up the nerve to approach the handsome blue-eyed tenor eleven years her senior. After Sunday services one afternoon, she coyly approached him and asked, "What time is it?" According to my mother's notes, Perry reached into his coat to retrieve his pocket watch. Handing Dorothy his timepiece, he answered her query by saying, "Here is my watch, and you have my heart as well."

After years on the road, with a marriage proposal on his mind, this "silver-tongued" cash register salesman was about to ring up the biggest sale of his life. I'm not sure how long their courtship lasted, but their plans for marriage hit a snag—Gottlieb Sturzinger, Dorothy's father. When Perry asked Gottlieb for his daughter's hand in marriage, the cantankerous old German immigrant would not consent—unless Perry agreed to take over running the Sturzinger farm. Already attending to his aging parents' farm, Perry must have had concerns about taking on an additional farming enterprise.

Anxious for Perry to gain her father's approval, Dorothy had an idea. After my mother died in 1990, I discovered a handwritten note buried in a box of papers. Mom's jottings said her mother Dorothy had "induced [Perry] to engage in market gardening," presumably as a way for him to take over her father's farm. Evidently the "inducement" worked, and Perry's soon-to-be father-in-law Gottlieb relented. The couple married on February 24, 1909, in Erie County. Perry was thirty-two, and his young bride, Dorothy, was twenty-one.

Dorothy and Perry Null with their young daughter, Virginia. Circa 1912.

Years later, *The Sandusky Register-Star News* reported that Perry conducted a successful truck farming business.[3] In a book titled *History of Ohio*, author Charles B. Galbreath says Perry owned his own market garden and contracted with commercial establishments to deliver fresh vegetables. These fresh provisions were likely grown on Gottlieb's farm.[4]

More than two decades after his military service ended, Perry's life took an unexpected turn: he received an astonishing advancement in military rank, promoted from private to general in one fell swoop—albeit with a twenty-three-year lapse between events. On October 5, 1921, reported the *Sandusky Register*, Perry was appointed Commandant of the Ohio Soldiers' and Sailors' Home in Sandusky. With the stroke of Ohio Governor Harry L. Davis's pen, the former Army private was instantly elevated to Brigadier General Perry L. Null—one star handsomely resting on each of his shoulders.

General Perry L. Null, Commandant of the Ohio Soldiers' and Sailors' Home. Circa 1921.

Sitting on ninety acres, the veteran's facility he commanded was home to hundreds of Ohio Civil War veterans ranging in age from seventy to ninety-five. "These grizzled old heroes are just a remnant of the most loyal army of soldiers that ever struggled . . . for freedom," said Hewson L. Peeke, president of the Firelands Historical Society.[5] Also residing at the home were soldiers who fought in the Indian wars, the Mexican War, and later, the Spanish-American War.

At the same time Perry became commandant, his wife Dorothy was appointed matron of the home. More than a ceremonial position created for a commandant's wife, the position was a hands-on job with wide-ranging responsibility, which entailed everything related to the well-being of her veterans. This included daily inspections of campus facilities, from the hospital and dining hall to the dormitories. She also oversaw the laundry department, the kitchen and food preparation, the cleaning crew, and the nursing staff who cared for the maladies of the former Union soldiers. In contemporary terms, she might be called the CCO (Chief Comfort Officer).

In addition to her duties at the Soldiers' Home, Dorothy was actively involved in community affairs. She was the first president of the Erie County Federation of Woman's Clubs and was later elected the first president of the Woman's Republican Club of Erie County. She probably rallied each of these organizations and other community assistance groups to provide service projects at the home for her veterans—all the while rearing two daughters: my mother, Virginia, and her sister, Doris.

As a Republican political appointee, Perry's job was on the line with each new administration. In those days, gubernatorial elections in Ohio were held every two years. He was able to weather four different governors: two Democrats and two Republicans. But the inevitability of political chicanery eventually ended his run at the helm of the Home.

Soon after Martin L. Davey's inauguration in January 1935, rumors began to swirl in Columbus that there would be a change in Sandusky. Finally, the whispers of a possible replacement at the Soldiers' Home surfaced on the front page of Sandusky's *The Star Journal* on July 23, 1935. The headline read, "Change at [Soldiers'] Home Said Certainty." The article stated: "Governor Davey will give the world for a change [at the Soldiers' Home] if there is sufficient basis for removal." The die was cast.

Nearly three months later, on October 15, 1935, another front-page article in *The Star Journal* reported, "It was learned from an authoritative source that strong pressure has been brought to bear on Governor Davey to 'lay off Null' [in] an effort . . . to secure the Home job for a Democrat."

A short time later, accusations started to emerge—right on cue. Leading the charge, the assistant state welfare director called the Home's veterans a "bunch of lazy whelps." When the Soldiers' Home first opened its doors, some of the routine maintenance work on the grounds was done by its residents—mostly Civil War veterans. With their advancing age and diminished physical abilities, they were later replaced by trustees from the Mansfield Reformatory. A penal institution, Mansfield was about forty-seven miles south of Sandusky. The practice of using its trustees for labor was in place long before Perry was appointed commandant.

The welfare agency charged that Null should have ended that practice and required younger residents—including veterans of the World War—to do the physical labor needed to keep up the grounds. The agency alleged his "mismanagement" caused needless expense to the state of Ohio.

There were numerous vocal defenders of the Nulls, including most of the Home's residents, the local American Legion post adjacent to the Soldiers' Home, and others. But to no avail. After nearly fifteen years, he was discharged by Democrat Governor Davey on June 1, 1936.

Without so much as a hint of personal or financial gain in any of the accusations attributed to Perry or Dorothy Null, this was clearly a political "hit job." Governor Davey was a ruthless operator by almost anyone's definition, and his administration was rife with accusations of corruption and retribution. According to a *Time* Magazine article on March 25, 1935, President "Franklin Roosevelt . . . on 'evidence concerning corrupt political interference with relief [funds] in the State of Ohio,' [ordered his advisor] Harry Hopkins to remove Democratic Governor Martin Luther Davey from all connection with Federal Relief Administration." In Hopkins's letter to the governor, he accused Davey of "shakedown" tactics to raise money to pay off his campaign and inauguration expenses. There were also accusations that "Mr. Davey had . . . wrecked a bank in his home town of Kent by approving excessive loans to himself."

The *National Governors Association* website further reveals that "Because of the scandals associated with his administration and New Deal maneuvering, Davey was defeated in the Democratic gubernatorial primary of 1938." In other words, his own party voted him off the ticket.

The protracted public flogging of the Nulls in the news media, initiated by Davey and his political cronies, left Perry and Dorothy stunned. In a letter to my mother, Dorothy wrote, "Daddy's resignation humiliated me more than anything that has ever happened to me." Several days later, the postman delivered another letter to my mother from her aunt, Bertha Null, Perry's sister. Bertha reveals in the letter that Dorothy told her the ordeal was "a sorrow next to death." In the blood sport of politics, Perry's trauma was no doubt the same.

On September 26, 1941, Perry and Dorothy headed north from their retirement home in New Port Richey, Florida. Given Perry's failing health, they were probably going to visit their daughters—Virginia and Doris—in Ohio and New York, when Perry suddenly passed away. The Army private and improbable general is buried on Lawton Drive, Section 22, in Arlington National Cemetery. Thirty-three years later, his wife Dorothy would join him there.

In spite of the deplorable treatment Perry received at the hands of the corrupt governor, the Null family has a proud history of service to our country. Perry's father, Levi, a private in Ohio's 35th Infantry Regiment, fought in some of the Civil War's bloodiest and most con-sequential battles. Perry's uncle, Joseph Null—Levi's brother—gave the ultimate sacrifice in that tragic war. And, on his mother's side, Perry's second great-grandfather, Ulrich Showalter, fought for our independence in the Revolution.

I always thought it curious that neither of my grandmothers wanted my brother Bob or me to call them Grandma. One insisted on being called Aunt Cora, while the other preferred Momma Dorothy. It was a different time in those days when women were more sensitive about their age. I guess it made them feel younger.

As for my grandfathers, both died before I was born. But despite never having their physical presence, I could feel their influence in my life through recollections of them passed down to me from my parents and grandmothers. They were God-fearing men, steeped in the Ger-man traditions of hard work, thrift, faith, and family.

In late August 2015, my wife Kathy and I started a three-week holiday traveling through western Europe. We took off from Philadelphia International Airport, landing in Brussels, Belgium, the next morn-ing. The following day, the first thing on our agenda was to head for Mettet, a tiny village about an hour's drive south of Brussels. Seventy-one years earlier, Kathy's dad was on the run in that locale, evading capture by the Germans. Our aim that day was to retrace some of her father's footsteps.

Walter P. McHugh—known as "Mac" to his friends—was a career soldier who served our country in World War II, the Korean War, and the Vietnam War. Prior to World War II, he was a professional baseball player with dreams of making it to "The Show."

After high school, Mac was signed by the old St. Louis Browns and entered their farm system, playing for the Findley (Ohio) Oilers.[6] After that, he bounced around the minor leagues as a player for several organizations. While on the Ogden Reds in Utah, a farm team in the Cincinnati Reds organization, Mac met Gloria Snively. She and her girlfriends often went to the ballpark after work to watch the Reds, and a handsome slugger named McHugh caught her eye. She was obviously taken by the tall Irishman who was voted "most popular Red" by the fans. In 1942, the Cincinnati Reds signed him as an outfielder for their Class B team, the Columbia Reds in South Carolina—and a year later, on November 22, 1943, Mac and Gloria were married.

Lt. Walter P. McHugh and his wife Gloria. Circa 1942.

Although Mac hoped to receive a call from the mother team in

Cincinnati and gain his ticket to the majors, World War II interrupted his plans. In the fall of 1942, Mac enlisted in what was then called the Army Air Corps (later renamed the United States Air Force)[7] where he trained to be a navigator on a B-24 bomber.

In his book, *With the Help of Strangers*, Kathy's brother Terry gives the harrowing account of what happened to their father on the fateful date of Wednesday, April 12, 1944.

With his ten-member crew, Mac left an air base in England on his 9th mission. Flying toward Germany, their heavy bomber was suddenly surrounded by a swarm of Luftwaffe fighters. With enemy machine guns blazing, Mac's plane had its controls and stabilizer shot away, with one engine feathered and another in trouble. Realizing his ship was critically damaged, the captain of the beleaguered plane knew what he had to do. At 10,000 feet, nearly two miles up, pilot John B. Anderson ordered his crew to abandon ship. Mac and four others bailed out through the nose hatch in the front of the plane while four bailed from a hatch in the rear.

With the crew clear, the hapless plane lumbered through the air, struggling to maintain altitude and air speed. Because the aircraft was still armed with a full load of fragmentation bombs, Anderson was in a desperate struggle to maneuver his doomed aircraft away from several small villages ahead. While floating toward Earth in his parachute, one of Anderson's crewmates watched his plane fall from the sky. "As the ship slowly lost altitude," he said, "I saw it crash into a field with the [full] bomb load."[8]

Hundreds of miles from their target in Germany and way off course, none of the airmen who escaped the crippled plane knew for sure where they were. All they had was their escape and evasion training—and their initiative and ingenuity.

Back home in Ogden, Mac's young wife Gloria was living with her mother and grandparents. Fifteen days after Mac's plane was attacked, a knock at the front door shook her world to its core. As it had for thousands of wives and families before her, the Western Union telegram carried the air of dreadful news. With tears probably welling in her eyes, Gloria opened the envelope.

> The Secretary of War desires me to express his deep regret that your husband, Second Lieutenant Walter P McHugh, has been reported missing in action since Twelve April over Germany. If further details or other information are received you will be promptly notified.

The agony of the excruciating wait was broken when reports from the War Department brought Gloria hopeful news. Other pilots in Mac's bomber group reported spotting parachutes in the sky as the crew bailed out of their injured Liberator. After-action reports from others in their squadron placed them over Belgium when they were attacked, not Germany as had been feared. A pilot in one of the other B-24s reported that Mac's plane was losing altitude and being strafed by enemy fighters near Malmedy, Belgium.[9]

Although Mac had landed safely on the ground, he was still in danger of being captured by the Nazis. His compass setting pointed him toward the French border. For four days, Mac kept to backroads and forests, drinking from streams. Finally, he made his way to Mesnil-Enlise, a village five miles from the French line. The town's mayor gave him food but sent him on his way. A few minutes later, another villager approached Mac and took him into hiding with another American flyer.

For the next 141 days, a small band of Belgian patriots, under risk of execution, shuffled the two fugitive airmen between private homes, farms, and an abandoned schoolhouse. This unlikely collection of heroes included a college professor, a couple of local citizens, several farmers, and the head of the local resistance organization and his wife.

After nearly five months on the run, thanks to the help of these strangers, Mac was liberated by advancing American troops on September 4, 1944. Ten days later, on September 14th, another Western Union telegram arrived at Gloria's doorstep on Brinker Avenue. With her heart likely pounding and hands trembling, she opened the envelope and read the following words: "Safe and well in Belgium. Wire Dad. Mac." This time, there were undoubtedly tears of joy.

Discharged on June 15, 1946, Mac enrolled at Idaho State University, earning a degree in Pharmacy in 1949. He worked as a pharmacist for two years, but in 1951, during the Korean War, he reenlisted as a lieutenant in the United States Air Force Medical Service Corps. Later, he earned a Master's Degree in Healthcare Administration from Baylor University. In addition to serving in Korea, his service included a tour in Vietnam in 1968 and 1969. He retired as a full colonel in 1975.

As for the strangers back in Belgium who risked their lives to save Mac and others, they were never far from Mac's thoughts. After the war, while stationed in Germany, he and Gloria visited them in their homes, and when my wife Kathy was twenty, she spent the summer in Ciney, Belgium, with the college professor and his family. In the late 1960s, the professor's daughter came to America to spend the summer with the McHugh family.

Today, in a farmer's field just outside of Mettet, Belgium, a monument marks the site of the crash. It pays homage to the brave pilot who sacrificed his life—and possibly even saved the town.

TIME ERASES NOTHING
PASSER-BY REMEMBER!

HERE DIED FOR OUR FREEDOM
AN AMERICAN PILOT OFFICER
IN HIS B24-J LIBERATOR.
445 BOMBER GROUP
701 SQUADRON
12 APR 1944

My father-in-law never mentioned his war experience to me, and I never brought it up. What little I knew about his ordeal I gleaned from my mother-in-law, Gloria, and more recently from Terry's book. Mac's best friend, General Don Wagner, delivered Mac's eulogy at the chapel at Fort Meyer. Beside the tiny sanctuary, just on the other side of a stone wall, lies Arlington National Cemetery. Mac and Gloria are buried in Section 64 on Bradley Drive, a short distance from my parents. In my view, it is altogether fit and proper that spouses share the same burial space as their veterans, as they serve our country, too, on the home front.

The final family member to have honorably served our country, and to be interred at Arlington, is my father, Robert W. Ruth.

In the summer of 1943, about a year and a half after the Japanese attack on Pearl Harbor, Dad joined the Navy. He spent most of that year and the next stationed in Washington, D.C., writing for the *Recognition Journal*, a Navy publication distributed to all of America's armed forces. A magazine that helped soldiers and sailors identify distant silhouettes of allied and enemy ships and aircraft, it was required reading for every front-line battle gunner. From ship or shore, the shooter had to distinguish friendly vessels and planes from enemy targets in a split second before pulling the trigger. A miscalculation would have tragic consequences.

The agonizing war that never seemed to end finally concluded in 1945 with a rapid surge of cascading developments. Dad described those events in Volume IV of *The Ruths,* the set of family history photo albums he assembled before his death.[10]

In April there was the shock of President Roosevelt's sudden death. Less than three weeks later Hitler, long doomed, ended his life [by] suicide in a Berlin bunker. The armistice was only days away, signed in May in the headquarters of Gen. Dwight D. Eisenhower at Reims, France. In early August [atomic] bombs devastated Hiroshima and Nagasaki. By mid-month Japan, threatened with total ruin, gave up on the demand of Emperor Hirohito [to remain in power as head of state]. On September 2 [1945] surrender ceremonies took place on the battleship Missouri in Tokyo harbor.

At last the massive killing that had overcome the world was over. People everywhere, even the vanquished, felt a great burden had been lifted. The victors danced in the streets at the news from Europe and Japan.

Less than three weeks after Japan's surrender, on September 21, 1945, my father's stateside duty ended. His new orders sent him to the Philippine Islands in the Pacific. Due to his background as a journalist, he was named managing editor of the *Navy News*. In Manila, he found a city "largely in ruins and . . . [a] harbor [that] was littered with bombed-out Japanese ships."[11]

In December of that year, Dad covered the war crimes trial of Japanese General Tomoyuki Yamashita. The soldiers under the general's command indiscriminately committed atrocities against civilians, enemy combatants, and prisoners of war alike. My father said Yamashita stood "emotionless" in front of a US military commission as he was pronounced guilty on December 8, 1945. His sentence—death by hanging—was carried out in early 1946. The Japanese general's trial set a precedent for judging command responsibility for war crimes, which still stands to this day.

Five months after he arrived in the Philippines, my father returned to Washington—one day before my birth on February 27, 1946.

A decade prior—one year after he and his friend Charlie Schmidt spent their summer in Europe—Dad had moved to Cleveland, Ohio, where he took his first job in journalism as a financial reporter for the *Cleveland News*. He bunked at a place called the Albion Club—a fancy name for a three-story, red-brick apartment house for young working singles. Women were housed on the second floor, while men were relegated to the third. The "club," once the mansion of paint magnate Sherwin Williams, had long since been converted into apartments.

One Saturday evening in February 1937, Dad was headed upstairs when he bumped into two female residents. One was a young school teacher named Virginia Null. She and her friend Kate were "standing on the stairway landing, halfway between the first and second floors," said my father in Volume III of his photo album. The two new friends hung out together regularly over the next two years, but this budding relationship would take some time to bloom.

In August 1939, Dad departed Cleveland for good and Virginia soon left for Boston.[12] Dad went to Washington, D.C., where his mother lived, and where he took a copyediting job at the *Baltimore*

Sun the following year. I'm not sure what prompted Virginia's move to Boston, but she returned to Cleveland a year or so later, where she accepted a job in nearby Euclid as the music supervisor for their schools.

Despite being separated by over 300 miles, the couple's romance continued to percolate on and off over the next couple of years. Periodically, they would link up for travel excursions—sometimes in the US and, on several occasions, north of the border. Virginia was a frequent guest at the Canadian cottage her sister Doris and husband Nelson Bell rented each summer, not far from Niagara Falls. In 1938 and 1939, Dad visited his sweetheart several times.[13]

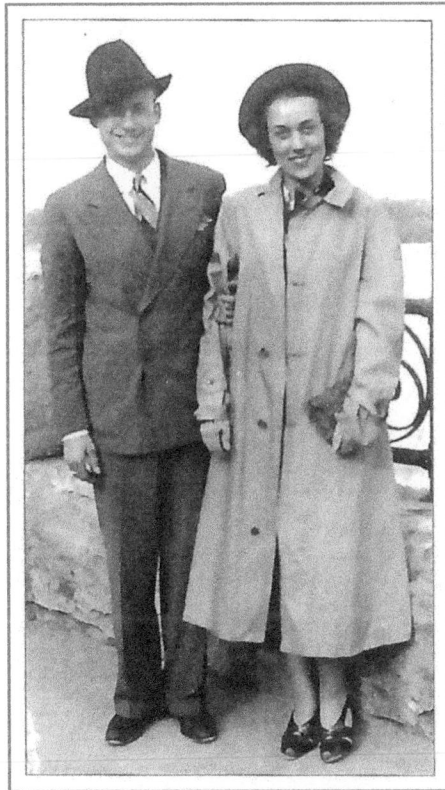

Robert Ruth and Virginia Null at Niagara Falls, New York, in 1938.

Finally, after nearly three years, their long-distance romance came to fruition. Robert and Virginia were married on May 23, 1942, in Washington, D.C. at the Church of the Covenant – First Presbyterian Church, where Dad had attended Sunday school as a child and where his father had been an elder. After a honeymoon in Mexico, they settled down in an apartment house in Baltimore, about a mile from Dad's work at the *Baltimore Sun*.[14]

Mom and Dad's marriage linked two families steeped in old-school German values. Both recognized the importance of education going back generations, and my parents were beneficiaries of that heritage. All four of their parents had attended college, an unusual occurrence for that time in America. Following in the footsteps of her mother, Dorothy, Mom received a degree in music from the Conservatory of Cincinnati and went into teaching. Her first assignment was in 1934: a fourth-grade class at Campbell School in Sandusky. Dad earned a Bachelor's degree from Washington and Lee University in Lexington, Virginia, south of his home in D.C.

With the war over and his military service behind him, Dad—with Mom, my brother Bobby, and one-year-old me in tow—returned to Maryland in 1947 to reclaim his job as a reporter for the *Baltimore Sun*. Soon after, the *Sun* transferred him to its Washington, D.C., bureau. Like his father before him, Dad's assignment was the White House and national politics. In 1955, he joined *US News and World Report* magazine as its political editor and White House correspondent.

By this time, my parents had moved to the suburbs in Bethesda, Maryland—an easy thirty-minute commute to Dad's office in nearby D.C. While my father was reporting politics, Mom had her hands full raising Bobby and me. How she managed to find time to give music lessons to children in our Locust Hills neighborhood while trying to keep her mischievous sons out of trouble, I'll never know.

I vividly remember the annual piano recitals Mom staged in our living room. The "theater" was created with extra chairs from the dining room and folding chairs retrieved from the basement, all of which were placed in rows beside the sofa and armchairs. Parents flocked to our house on Locust Hill Road at the appointed time for a standing-room-only crowd. Bounding up our front porch steps, musical prodigies in hand, the proud parents were trailed by herds of brothers and sisters. Mesmerized toddlers sat cross-legged on the floor, watching their older siblings pound out melodies on the ivory keys of Mom's Steinway. It was a spectacle that delighted all.

Back on the Washington scene, Dad wrote stories about the five presidents he covered: Harry Truman, Dwight Eisenhower, John Kennedy, Lyndon Johnson, and Richard Nixon. He had an exciting career with a close-up view of the world during tumultuous times—but reporting the politics of Washington and the world is a demanding line of work. Cynicism is an occupational hazard and eventually, it took its toll on him.

Some years later, he told me that "Politics is prostitution." There were only two political figures, he said, over all those years, who were genuine human beings. While he disagreed with the politics of one, both were authentic people he liked and trusted. One was former vice-president and Democrat presidential hopeful Hubert Humphrey. The other, a Republican, would later become President Gerald Ford. All the others, he said, "wore masks," concealing their true identity.

He walked away from political reporting without regret in 1973, just as President Nixon's Watergate scandal was heating up. He was sixty-one when he retired to pursue other interests, years earlier than most of his colleagues in the Washington press corps.

After nearly thirty years in Bethesda, my parents moved to Florida around 1974. Mom passed away some sixteen years later, in 1990. Dad followed ten years after that, in 2000. They are buried together at Arlington in the columbarium on Bradley Drive, Court #3, Section 3B.

In the fall of 2006, I was in downtown Washington, D.C. for a morning of business appointments. Before returning to my office in the Maryland suburbs, I pointed my car toward Arlington National Cemetery. If I hurried, I'd have just enough time to make the rounds of our family graves.

After bailing out my car from a parking garage on 14th Street, I drove to Constitution Avenue, picking up the road that circles the Lincoln Memorial. On the far side of the monument, a sharp right-hand turn took me across Memorial Bridge over the Potomac River. Straight ahead was Arlington. As my car rolled past the visitor's entrance, I flashed my family pass to the guard, who waved me on. From there, my car was virtually on autopilot. My hands instinctively turned the steering wheel left on Eisenhower Drive, then continued four or five blocks before making another left on Bradley Drive.

Just ahead was my parents' grave—but my plan to visit the relatives was interrupted when I saw a funeral in progress. As I approached, I nudged my car to the curb, getting as close as possible without intruding. From where I was parked, I saw six soldiers outfitted in crisp dress blues. In lockstep, they bore a flag-draped casket across a freshly manicured lawn to its final resting place, a nearby gravesite. An Army chaplain conducted a brief service lasting maybe fifteen or twenty minutes. I was too far away to hear the words he spoke, but I knew that the sound of his voice and the message it conveyed comforted the family.

As the chaplain stepped aside, the family rose from their chairs. A firing party raised their rifles, shooting volleys toward the sky. A bugler played taps as soldiers removed the American flag that had draped the casket. The stars and stripes were crisply tri-folded with precision. A waiting officer received the flag and reverently handed it to the soldier's widow. As the small crowd of mourners dispersed, I reached for the ignition key and pointed my car toward home. Visiting my relatives would have to wait for another day.

Several days after the funeral, I discovered that the young soldier was killed in action in the war in Iraq. As I sat silently in my car that afternoon, glassy-eyed with emotion, thoughts raced through my head. I was thankful this young American hero could be laid to rest in this special place with his brothers and sisters in arms—and I was reminded again that Arlington is not only for our nation's political and military leaders. It is populated primarily with ordinary soldiers, sailors, Marines, Air Force personnel, and Coast Guard members who have served our country.

Only a fraction of the three million visitors to Arlington each year are family members of the 400,000-plus veterans who are buried there. But there is something about this place most tourists wandering the grounds of the nation's cemetery don't understand. Arlington is not merely a place to bury our honored dead; it's for the living, too—the ones left behind. That young soldier's wife and their two small sons will forever have this hallowed ground to comfort their hearts—a place to rekindle fading memories of what was and to imagine a life that could have been.

I try not to live in the past, but I find the memories of my yesterdays become more precious as the years go by. The 639 acres of sacred ground at Arlington safeguard an honored part of my family's heritage—but it's not where the Ruth's American journey ends. It's where the next chapters begin. They will be written by my children, Heather and Michael; my grandsons Matthew and Andrew; my brother Bob's kids, John, Cindy, and Diane's son Ian. It will continue with their children and their cousins, and other family descendants—all in pursuit of life, liberty and happiness in America.

These future Ruths will undoubtedly experience their own triumphs and hardships, just as their ancestors did. They will celebrate the highs and soldier on through the lows. That's the story of the Ruths, the story of America.

Now, in my seventy-eighth year, I still dutifully make the rounds of our family memorials at Arlington—my heart overflowing with gratitude and admiration at each headstone. Only now, the long arc of my thoughts, spanning nearly 300 years, is with me at each stop.

Reaching out to touch the white marble stones, I feel the spirit of Peter, Sophia, Catharine, and all the others who followed. I try to imagine what they would think and what they might say if they were standing here beside me—looking back all those years ago to 1733 when they came to America.

Maybe, contemplating the legacy their cascading ripples etched in our lives, they might echo the words of the Congressional tribute to my grandfather, Carl, and simply say, *"Es gibt Zeiten, in denen die Zunge die Sprache des Herzens nicht sprechen kann."*

"There are times when the tongue cannot speak the language of the heart."

Sundown at Arlington National Cemetery.
Photo courtesy of ANC from their website.

AFTERWORD

About fifteen years ago, my wife Kathy and I located the stone house Peter built, the same one we visited at the reunion in 1983 and that left an indelible impression on me. Turning right off Route 422 onto a private one-lane road, we stealthily headed toward the residence in the distance. About three-quarters of the way down the long drive, I pulled my car off to the side, two wheels resting on the grass. The clearing gave me a good view of the house, some 300 yards away. The description of the home, taken from the 1916 *History of the St. John's (Hain's) Reformed Church,* still rang true:

> Behind the imposing home were gently rising hills in the distant background crowned in the highest point with a group of stately old chestnut trees, all combined to make of this homestead a picture of peace, plenty and content that it would be hard to surpass anywhere.

I got out of the car and snapped a few quick pictures. Though built nearly 300 years ago, it was beautifully preserved and restored, just as I remembered from my 1983 visit.

As I was about to turn the car around and head back to the highway, the current homeowner spotted us and hurriedly pulled his car beside ours. Through his open window, he rudely proclaimed, "You're on private property!" I tried to explain why we were there, but it made little difference. He implied that the Ruths are a nosy clan. Apparently,

Kathy and I weren't the first Ruths to venture down this long driveway and "trespass" on his land.

As we pulled away, I told Kathy, "If I ever win the lottery, I'm gonna make this guy an offer he can't refuse."

Alas, the lottery win hasn't occurred—not yet. But if it ever does, you can bet I will make that offer. I can think of no better way to honor my fifth great-grandfather—the man who gave up everything with such courage and optimism to seek a life without political or religious persecution in a new and unfamiliar land—than to reclaim the homestead he built with his own hands for future Ruth generations to come.

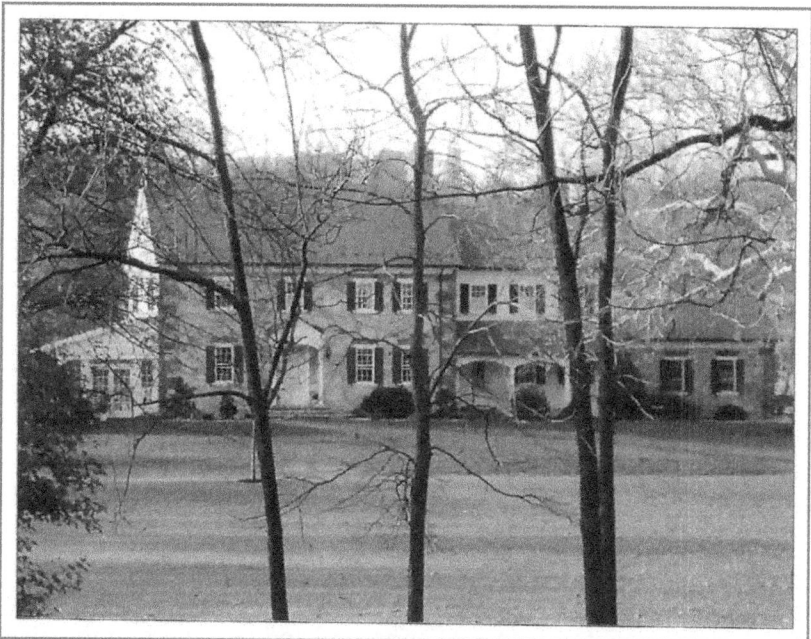

The Ruth mansion on a branch of the Cacoosing Creek.
Photo by the author, Jim Ruth.

ACKNOWLEDGMENTS

It is impossible to take on a project of this scope and magnitude without the help of others. There are numerous people, institutions, and organizations I leaned on to complete my self-appointed task of telling the family story of the Ruths—one spanning nearly 300 years. Many people unselfishly gave me the benefit of their time, recollections, opinions, and editorial insight. Even their criticisms, artfully couched as suggestions, were much appreciated.

This sentimental, historical journey would not have been possible without my wife, Kathy Ruth. A decade before I decided to take on this project, she started the process of discovering, documenting, and preserving Ruth family history and artifacts on Ancestry.com. Her interest and dedication helped spark my curiosity, eventually fueling my desire to dive deeply into my family history. Little did I realize then that interest would spawn a historical biography about my ancestors.

Although I am an experienced writer of articles, I am a novice writer of books. I didn't know what I didn't know, and I had a lot to learn. My older brother, Bob Ruth, gave me a crash course in grammar, gently schooling me in the art of keeping verb tenses consistent and a myriad of other finer points of the English language previously ignored by me. Brother Bob is a retired journalist and Civil War historian. His latest writing endeavor, *The General's Navy*, is a trailblazing book about General Ulysses S. Grant's strategic use of naval forces in the Civil War.

I am indebted to my dad, Robert Ruth, for leaving a collection of family documents, stories, and images. In the 1990s, he assembled a set of five family history albums titled *The Ruths*. Every page was crammed with family photographs, each with identifying captions or short narrative descriptions about family life and the times in which they lived. Some pages contained colorfully illustrated maps drawn by Dad, while others were photocopies of newspaper front pages highlighting momentous world events.

My childhood friend, John Conradis, was among the first people I contacted for help with my fledgling journalistic venture. Our friendship predates kindergarten, going back to the early 1950s. He read the first two chapters of *The Pursuit* and gave me encouragement up until his untimely death in the fall of 2022. Known as Jaycee in our youth, he was probably my oldest friend. A patriot, American history scholar, and prolific author, Jaycee also referred me to a potential publisher, resulting in my first publishing contract offer. I am forever in his debt.

Perched atop the list of extended family members who were instrumental in writing *The Pursuit* sits second cousin, Steve Smith. His knowledge of family history was essential in unlocking a trove of documents buried deep in widely scattered family archives. Steve also knew the supporting cast of past and present characters who accumulated and preserved archival records: folks like Esther Ruth Smith, Ruth Annetta King, Ruth Annetta Smith King, and Betty J. Hartley. Steve also graciously read one of the chapters, contributing valuable ideas and essential details. It is hard to imagine this project coming to fruition without his help.

Rebecca Eddy was another "cousin" who unselfishly reviewed several chapters, supplying valuable insight and additional family lore. Also stepping up to the plate was extended family cousin Mary Parsons, who delivered a wealth of ancestral intelligence and a trove of family tales and documents.

Another early contributor was my neighbor (at the time), Lisa Graff. An accomplished author herself, Lisa unselfishly reviewed one of my early chapters and offered encouragement just when I needed it most. She told me, "This is a gift to yourself, as well as to your family."

While researching family patriarch Peter Ruth's settlement in eastern Pennsylvania, I stumbled on an authentic Pennsylvania Dutchman, Tom Gerhart. He's the longtime president of the 132-year-old Pennsylvania German Society. Coincidentally, this eighth-generation Pennsylvania Dutchman is also a descendant of Peter Ruth. Cousin Tom invited me to his farm in the summer of 2021 to view his collection of colonial Pennsylvania memorabilia. He and his wife Judy were gracious hosts, sharing their massive assemblage of Ruth/Gerhart documents, books, and relics—small world.

Before submitting my manuscript to a publisher, I hired an independent editor, Brooke Maddaford, at Word Hawk Editing in Denver, Colorado. She was thoughtful and patient, and her line editing helped immensely in the first draft of my manuscript. I also received an assist from book coach and prolific author Kathryn Johnson in Silver Spring, Maryland, who offered valuable insight and helped me sort through the whole publishing maze. And finally, with my publisher secured, I was lucky to have Stacey Aaronson as my book doctor for the final lap of this endeavor. Her editing prowess, book layout and design skills, and publishing expertise finally brought *The Pursuit* across the finish line.

There were also several organizations or institutions that went beyond the call of duty to help me tell my family story. I frequently consulted The Pennsylvania German Society's collection of books and articles detailing early Pennsylvania Dutch people and life. They were regularly noted as a primary source for my research. While living in Lewes, Delaware, the Lewes Public Library was a vital source of historical books and documents, often having them shipped in from other libraries for my review.

And then, there are the folks at the Lewes Historical Society. This dedicated group of scholars offered a wealth of historical information about the colonial town that bears its name. Archivist Denise Clemons was incredibly generous with her time when this project was in its infancy. She assembled historic documents for my review and directed me to additional resources to pursue in my quest for information. Another invaluable source was Hathi Trust. This international consortium of online libraries offers access to nearly 14 million volumes of old books, digitized for public access. I was a frequent visitor to their site.

To all of the people and organizations who helped me follow the trail of breadcrumbs left by my ancestors, you have my admiration and gratitude. I couldn't have done it without you.

NOTES

CHAPTER ONE
The Reunion

[1] Kathy Ruth, "Ruth Null Family Tree," *Ancestry*, www.ancestry.com/search. (Documents and records stored under Johann Peter Ruth in Kathy Ruth's account in the Gallery section regarding the 1983 250th Anniversary Reunion of his coming to America.)

[2] Anonymous, "Handout Materials," *Ruth Reunion – 250th Anniversary of Peter Ruth Coming to America*, (September 17–19, 1983). Materials distributed to attendees included itinerary, description of various Ruth properties, maps, land surveys, land grant indentures, estate settlement petition, and miscellaneous other documents. Copies are in the possession of the author, Thomas Gerhart, president of the Pennsylvania German Society, and other family attendees.

[3] Ibid.

[4] W.J. Kershner and Adam G. Lerch, *History of St. John's (Hain's) Reformed Church* (Reading, Pennsylvania: I.M. Beaver, 1916), 2, 10–11, 13, 15, 18–19, 460–61, 467–68.

[5] Anonymous, *Saint John's United Church of Christ*, 1992 – 200th Anniversary Edition (Sinking Spring: St. John's United Church of Christ, 1992), 3, 8.

[6] Lawrence Knorr, writing in *Der Reggeboge,* the Journal of the Pennsylvania German Society, 2014, 51, 58.

[7] Anonymous, *Saint John's United Church of Christ.*

[8] Committee appointed by Consistory, *History of St. John's (Hain's) Reformed Church of Lower Heidelberg Township, Berks County, Pennsylvania – Bicentennial Supplement 1935.* (United States: Intell. Ptg. Company, 1935), 210.

———

CHAPTER TWO
The Crossing: Braving Land and Sea

[1] Emilie Dosquet, "We have been Informed that the French are Carrying Desolation Everywhere: The Desolation of the Palatinate as a European News Event," *News Networks in Early Modern Europe,* ed Joad Raymond and Noah Moxham (Leiden/Boston: Brill, downloaded July 22, 2021) Chapter 28, 642, 643. www.jstor.org/action/doBasicSearch?Query=we+have+been+informed+that+the+french.

[2] Jack Akerboom and Anna Ruth Salzman, *The Descendants of Peter and Sophia (Lauer) Ruth*, (Elverson, Pennsylvania: Mennonite Family History, 1994), iv. Note:

Conflicting historical records say Christian was age four, so it isn't known for certain if the boys were twins or not.

[3] David Scholtze, "Narrative of the Journey of the Schwenckfelders to Pennsylvania, 1733," *The Pennsylvania Magazine of History and Biography*, Vol. 10, July, 1886, 171, 173–75, 177, 178.

[4] Ibid.

[5] Farley Grubb, "The Market Structure of Shipping German Immigrants to Colonial America," *The Pennsylvania Magazine of History and Biography*, Vol. 111, no. 1, (January, 1987), 47.

[6] Anonymous, *Minutes of the Provincial Council of Pennsylvania* – Vol. 3, (Harrisburg: Theophilus Penn, 1840), 557.

[7] David Scholtze, "Narrative of the Journey."

[8] "Nun lasst uns den Leib begraben" (Now Let Us Bury the Body) was a Lutheran hymn customarily sung at funerals. It was written by theologian Michael Weiße with a melody by Johann Sebastian Bach.

[9] David Scholtze, "Narrative of the Journey."

[10] Ibid.

[11] Johannes (John) Naas, "The John Naas Letter – A 1733 Crossing in the Pennsylvania Merchant," *Bushong United*, assessed June 15, 2023, www.belizebreeze.com/bushongunited/naas.html.

[12] David Scholtze, "Narrative of the Journey."

[13] Ibid.

[14] Klaus Wust, "Feeding the Palatines: Shipboard Diet in the Eighteenth Century," *The Report of Society for the History of Germans in Maryland* Vol. 39, (1984), 32. https://loyolanotredamelib.org/php/report05/articles/pdfs/Report39Wustp32-42.pdf.

[15] Ibid.

[16] Johannes (John) Naas, "The John Naas Letter."

[17] Ibid.

[18] Ibid.

[19] Ralph Beaver Strassburger, *Pennsylvania German Pioneers*, Vol. 1, (Norristown, PA: Pennsylvania German Society, 1934), xxxii-xxxv.

[20] Anonymous, "Navigation: The Mariner's Quadrant," *Ponce Inlet Lighthouse and Museum*, 2, assessed June 16, 2023, https://www.ponceinlet.org/z/-vf.0.0.0.190.C46 BA4D37972D11A71835BC2E31E574BAAAEFEABBCE8B82CA6E1356E6E889D60.

[21] Johannes (John) Naas, "The John Naas Letter."

[22] Ralph Beaver Strassburger, *Pennsylvania German Pioneers*, Vol. 1, (Norristown, PA: Pennsylvania German Society, 1934), xxxii-xxxv.

[23] Johannes (John) Naas, "The John Naas Letter."

[24] David Scholtze, "Narrative of the Journey."

[25] Johannes (John) Naas, "The John Naas Letter."

CHAPTER THREE
Land Ho – The Delaware: From Daydream to Reality

[1] Johannes (John) Naas, "The John Naas Letter – A 1733 Crossing in the Pennsylvania Merchant," *Bushong United*, assessed June 15, 2023, www.belizebreeze.com/bushongunited/naas.html.

[2] David Scholtze (Shults), "Narrative of the Journey of the Schwenckfelders to Pennsylvania, 1733," *The Pennsylvania Magazine of History and Biography*, Vol. 10, 1886, 167-179. http://wvancestry.com/ReferenceMaterial/Files/The_Pennsylvania_Magazine_of_History_and_Biography_Vol_10.pdf.

[3] Johannes (John) Naas, "The John Naas Letter."

[4] David Scholtze (Shults), "Narrative of the Journey of the Schwenckfelders to Pennsylvania, 1733."

[5] Johannes (John) Naas, "The John Naas Letter."

[6] David Scholtze (Shults), "Narrative of the Journey of the Schwenckfelders to Pennsylvania, 1733."

[7] Johannes (John) Naas, "The John Naas Letter."

[8] Dick Carter, *History of Sussex County* (United States: Community Newspaper Corporation, 1976), 3–5, 10, 11.

[9] Ibid.

[10] Jennifer Ackerman, "A Seafaring Town in Delaware," *New York Times*, June 21, 1992, Section 5, 18.

[11] Bob Kotowski, "A City of Two Tales: The Unsolved Mystery of the Swanendael Massacre," *Journal of the Lewes Historical Society* 21 (2018): 24.

[12] Virginia Cullen, *History of Lewes, Delaware*, (Lewes and Rehoboth Hundred: Colonel David Hall Chapter, National Society, Daughters of the American Revolution, 1956) 12, 16.

[13] Anonymous, "Colonial America, The Colonies – Delaware [Est. 1638]," *Small Planet*, accessed June 13, 2023, http://www.smplanet.com/teaching/colonialamerica/colonies/delaware.

[14] Harold B. Hancock, *The History of Sussex County, Delaware* (United States: Self-Published, 1976) 12, 21–23, 26, 30.

[15] Virginia Cullen, *History of Lewes, Delaware.*

[16] C.H.B. Turner, *Some Records of Sussex County Delaware* (Philadelphia: Allen, Lane and Scott, 1909), 2, 6.

[17] Harold B. Hancock, *The History of Sussex County, Delaware.*

[18] Ibid.

[19] Michael Schreiber, "Philadelphia's Rich Maritime History," *Founders Magazine*, Spring 2020, 4, 5, 15.

[20] David Marine, "Duke of York Patents on Pilottown Road," *The Archeolog – Publication of the Sussex Archaeological Association* 7, no. 2 (1955): 1.

[21] Ibid.

[22] Dick Carter, *History of Sussex County.*

[23] C.H.B. Turner, *Some Records of Sussex County Delaware.*

[24] Harold B. Hancock, *The History of Sussex County, Delaware.*

[25] Ibid.

[26] Ibid.

[27] Johannes (John) Naas, "The John Naas Letter."

[28] David Scholtze (Shults), "Narrative of the Journey of the Schwenckfelders to Pennsylvania, 1733."

[29] Farley Grubb, "The Market Structure of Shipping German Immigrants to Colonial America," *The Pennsylvania Magazine of History and Biography*, 111, no. 1 (1987): 37, 42.

[30] Ibid.

[31] Johannes (John) Naas, "The John Naas Letter."

[32] Ibid.

[33] David Scholtze (Shults), "Narrative of the Journey of the Schwenckfelders to Pennsylvania, 1733."

[34] Michael Schreiber, "Philadelphia's Rich Maritime History."

[35] Arthur L. Jensen, *The Maritime Commerce of Colonial Philadelphia* (Madison: The State Historical Society of Wisconsin for the Department of History, University of Wisconsin, 1963), 7.

[36] David Scholtze (Shults), "Narrative of the Journey of the Schwenckfelders to Pennsylvania, 1733."

[37] State of Pennsylvania, *Minutes of the Provincial Council of Pennsylvania*, Vol. 3 (Harrisburg: Theophilus Penn, 1840), 557.

[38] Ralph Beaver Strassburger, *Pennsylvania German Pioneers*, Vol. 1 (Norristown: Pennsylvania German Society, 1934), viii, ix.

———

CHAPTER FOUR
The Settling: Pennsylvania Dutch Country

[1] Ralph Beaver Strassburger, *Pennsylvania German Pioneers*, (Norristown, Pennsylvania: Pennsylvania German Society, 1934), Vol. I, vii.

[2] Oswald Seidenstricker, "William Penn's Travels in Holland and Germany in 1677," *The Pennsylvania Magazine of History and Biography*, Vol. II, No. 3 (1878): 237, 239.

[3] Ibid.

[4] W.J. Kershner and Adam G. Lerch, *History of St. John's (Hain's) Reformed Church* (Reading, Pennsylvania: I.M. Beaver, 1916), 2, 10–11, 13, 15, 18–19, 460–61, 467–68.

[5] Kathy Ruth, "Ruth-Null Family Tree," *Ancestry*, (Documents stored under Johann Peter Ruth in the Gallery section regarding the 1983, 250th Anniversary Reunion of his coming to America. An address by John Lowry Ruth to the Ruth Family Association of Illinois at the first annual reunion of the association, August 29, 1936.) www.ancestry.com/search.

[6] Paul A. W. Wallace, "Historic Indian Paths of Pennsylvania," *The Pennsylvania Magazine of History and Biography*, 76, no. 4 (October, 1952): 414, 416, 434.

[7] Kathy Ruth, "Ruth-Null Family Tree."

[8] Sharon A. Brown, "Southeastern Pennsylvania Agricultural Practices – Historic Resource Study Slateford Farm," *National Park Service*, last updated December 31, 2009, accessed September 18, 2023.

[9] Ibid.

[10] Anonymous, "Handout Materials," *Ruth Reunion – 250th Anniversary of Peter Ruth Coming to America*, (September 17–19, 1983), Materials distributed to attendees include itinerary, description of various Ruth properties, maps, land surveys, land grant indentures, estate settlement petition and miscellaneous other documents. Copies are in the possession of the author, Thomas Gerhart, president of the Pennsylvania German Society, and other family attendees.

[11] Cyrus T. Fox, *Reading and Berks County Pennsylvania: A History*, Vol I (New York: Lewis Historical Publishing Company, 1925), 10–11, 18–19, 101–02, 234, 469, 545; Vol. III, 422.

[12] Katelyn M. Miller, "American-Germans or German Americans?: Defining the Pennsylvania Dutch, 1891–1918," *American University Digital Research Archive*, Spring, 2010, 3.

[13] Cyrus T. Fox, *Reading and Berks County Pennsylvania.*

[14] W.J. Kershner and Adam G. Lerch, *History of St. John's (Hain's) Reformed Church.*

[15] Jack Akerboom and Anna Ruth Salzman, *The Descendants of Peter and Sophia (Lauer) Ruth*, (Elverson, Pennsylvania: Mennonite Family History, 1994), 10.

[16] John B. Linn and William H. Egle, *Pennsylvania Archives, Second Series*, Vol. II (Harrisburg: B.F Meyers, State Printer, 1876), 347, 410–11.

[17] Committee appointed by Consistory, *History of St. John's (Hain's) Reformed Church of Lower Heidelberg Township, Berks County, Pennsylvania – Bicentennial Supplement 1935*. (United States: Intell. Ptg. Company, 1935), 208.

[18] Cyrus T. Fox, *Reading and Berks County Pennsylvania*.

[19] Joseph S. Walton, *Conrad Weiser and the Indian Policy of Colonial Pennsylvania*, (Philadelphia: George W. Jacobs & Company, 1900), 13.

[20] Cyrus T. Fox, *Reading and Berks County Pennsylvania*.

[21] David Venditta, "We Are Now the Frontier," *The Morning Call* (Allentown, PA) November 26, 2006, accessed September 19, 2023, https://www.mcall.com/news/all-fi_mayhemnov26-story.html.

[22] George A. Bray III, "Scalping During the French and Indian War," *Varsity Tutors*, accessed June 7, 2023, www.varsitytutors.com/earlyamerica/early-america-review/volume-3/scalping-during-the-french-and-indian-war.

[23] David Venditta, "We Are Now the Frontier."

[24] W.J. Kershner and Adam G. Lerch, *History of St. John's (Hain's) Reformed Church*.

[25] Cyrus T. Fox, *Reading and Berks County Pennsylvania*.

[26] W.J. Kershner and Adam G. Lerch, *History of St. John's (Hain's) Reformed Church*.

[27] Cyrus T. Fox, *Reading and Berks County Pennsylvania*.

[28] Minnie F. Mickley, The Genealogy of the Mickley Family of America (Mickleys, Pennsylvania: Publisher Unknown,1893), 15, 16.

————

CHAPTER FIVE

The Revolution: Life, Liberty, and The Pursuit

[1] James Fritz, *The Pennsylvania Dutch Experience 1681–1783*, (Ephrata, Pennsylvania: Pennsylvania German Society, 2019), 5.

[2] Agricola, "To the Printer," *The Pennsylvania Packet*, April 24, 1781, 1.

[3] Anonymous, "Lexington and Concord," *American Battlefield Trust*, accessed June 18, 2023, www.battlefields.org/learn/revolutionary-war/battles/lexington-and-concord.

[4] Elizabeth Nix, "What was the 'shot heard round the world'?," *History*, last modified August 30, 2018, www.history.com/news/what-was-the-shot-heard-round-the-world.

5 Ibid.

6 Ibid.

7 Anonymous, Rolls and Lists of Connecticut Men in the Revolution (Hartford: Connecticut Historical Society, 1901), 5.

8 James Clark, "Lexington Alarm, accounts of Captain James Clark, 1775," American Revolution Collection, accessed April 1, 2024. https://digitalcatalog.chs.org/islandora/object/40002%3A5161#page/1/mode/1up.

9 William R. Cutter, New England Families – Third Series, Vol I (New York: Lewis Historical Publishing Company, 1915), 434.

10 Ibid.

11 Secretary of the Commonwealth, Massachusetts Soldiers and Sailors of the Revolutionary War (Boston: Wright and Potter Printing Company, 1905), 440.

12 Katelyn M. Miller, "American-Germans or German Americans?: Defining the Pennsylvania Dutch, 1891-1918," American University Digital Research Archive, Spring, 2010, 4, https://dra.american.edu/islandora/object/0910capstones%3A85.

13 Dean Snow, "Continental and Militia Cavalry Compared: A Case Study From Saratoga, 1777," Journal of the American Revolution, August 31, 2021, accessed September 6, 2023, www.allthingsliberty.com/2021/08/continental-and-militia-cavalry-compared-a-case-study-from-saratoga-1777.

14 Steve Smith, "Major Elijah Hyde and Liberty," YouTube, December 8, 2018, accessed September 6, 2023, www.youtube.com/watch?v=AaT1jhyitrg.

15 Joseph Ross, "The History & People of the Continental Navy," ContinentalNavy.com, posted March 20, 2010, accessed September 10, 2023, (Ebenezer Hyde), http://continentalnavy.com/archives/2010/ebenezer-hyde-crewman/.

16 Dean Snow, "Continental and Militia Cavalry Compared."

17 Anonymous, "Battle of Saratoga," The Saratoga County Chamber, accessed June 18, 2023, www.saratoga.org/battle-of-saratoga.

18 Hoffman Nickerson, The Turning Point of the Revolution (Boston and New York: Houghton Mifflin Company, 1928), 353.

19 Anonymous, "Battle of Saratoga," The Saratoga County Chamber, accessed June 18, 2023, www.saratoga.org/battle-of-saratoga.

20 Eric Schnitzer, "Battle of Saratoga: When Goliath Blinked," Hallowed Ground Magazine/American Battlefield Trust, last updated March 25, 2021, www.battlefields.org/learn/articles/battle-saratoga-when-goliath-blinked.

21 Steve Smith, "Major Elijah Hyde and Liberty."

22 Dean Snow, "Continental and Militia Cavalry Compared."

23 Wikipedia 2024, "Battles of Saratoga," Wikimedia Foundation, last modified May 25, 2024, at 19:27 (UTC), https://en.wikipedia.org/wiki/Battles_of_Saratoga.

[24] Harry Schenawolf, "Battle of Groton Heights and Massacre of Fort Griswold's Garrison," *Revolutionary War Journal*, July 16, 2021, accessed September 6, 2023, https://revolutionarywarjournal.com/battle-of-groton-heights-and-massacre-of-fort-griswolds-garrison/.

[25] Edward Baker, "Benedict Arnold Turns and Burns New London," *ConnecticutExplored.org*, Vol.4, No. 4, Fall 2006, accessed September 5, 2023 https://www.ctexplored.org/benedict-arnold-turns-and-burns-new-london/.

[26] Ibid.

[27] Ibid.

[28] Anonymous, *History of Wabasha County* (Chicago: H.H. Hill & Company, 1884), 952.

[29] Harry Schenawolf, "Battle of Groton Heights."

[30] Charles Allyn, *The Battle of Groton Heights* (New London, Connecticut: Charles Allyn, 1882), 17–20, 23, 25–28.

[31] Ibid.

[32] Ibid.

[33] Harry Schenawolf, "Battle of Groton Heights."

[34] Ibid.

[35] Charles Allyn, *The Battle of Groton Heights.*

[36] *Wikipedia* 2024, "Battle of Groton Heights," Wikimedia Foundation, last modified June 1, 2024, at 1:33 (UTC), https://en.wikipedia.org/wiki/Battle_of_Groton_Heights.

[37] Harry Schenawolf, "Battle of Groton Heights." and Charles Allyn, *The Battle of Groton Heights.*

[38] Harry Schenawolf, "Battle of Groton Heights."

[39] Charles Allyn, *The Battle of Groton Heights.*

[40] Ibid.

[41] Charles Henry James Douglas, *A Collection of Family Records with Biographical Sketches . . . Bearing the Name Douglas* (Providence: E. L. Freeman and Company, 1879), 75, 76, 93.

[42] Ibid.

[43] *Wikipedia* 2024, "Battle of Groton Heights."

[44] Joseph Ross, "The History & People of the Continental Navy."

[45] Christopher Hawkins and Charles I. Bushnell, *The Adventures of Christopher Hawkins* (New York, privately printed, 1864), 66, 67, 71, 213, 214, 216, 261–64, 267, 268, 284.

[46] Ibid.

———

CHAPTER SIX
The Fledgling Republic: A House Divided

[1] Geoffrey C. Ward, with Ric Burns and Ken Burns, *The Civil War* (New York: Alfred A. Knopf, 1990), XVI, XIX, 324.

[2] Ibid.

[3] W.J. Kershner and Adam G. Lerch, *History of St. John's (Hain's) Reformed Church* (Reading, Pennsylvania: I.M. Beaver, 1916), 49.

[4] Geoffrey C. Ward, with Ric Burns and Ken Burns, *The Civil War.*

[5] Tori Avey, *"Civil War Cooking: What the Union Soldiers Ate," PBS/The History Kitchen,* September 21, 2012, accessed September 7, 2023, www.pbs.org/food/the-history-kitchen/civil-war-cooking-what-the-union-soldiers-ate.

[6] Ibid.

[7] Ibid.

[8] Steve Smith, *Finding Benjamin Franklin Morse – Civil War Diary,* 1/25/2022. An article written by family genealogist, Steve Smith, to members of the Smith/Ruth family tree, containing transcriptions of various Benjamin Franklin Morse documents and letters including: his Civil War pocket diary, two letters Morse wrote to his father from the field, a sympathy letter from Sergeant J. S. Hedges, notifying his father, James Morse, of his son's death and Smith's historical narrative and interpretation of the events surrounding the life and death of the subject. The document is in the possession of Jim Ruth, Steve Smith and numerous other family members. Accessed September 7, 2023, file:///C:/Users/jruth/Downloads/Benjamin%20Morse%20Civil%20War%20 diary4.pdf.

[9] Tori Avey, *"Civil War Cooking: What the Union Soldiers Ate."*

[10] Steve Smith, *Finding Benjamin Franklin Morse.*

[11] Penrose G. Mark, *Red, White and Blue* (Harrisburg, Pennsylvania: Aughinbaugh Press, 1911) 148-153. Anonymous, "Rev. James M. McCarter," *Maryland State Archives (Biographical Series),* accessed September 7, 2023. https://msa.maryland.gov/megafile/msa/speccol/sc5400/sc5496/051500/051531/html/51531bio.html.

[12] Ibid, Anonymous.

[13] Penrose G. Mark, *Red, White and Blue.*

[14] Ibid.

[15] Ibid.

[16] Ibid.

[17] Ibid.

[18] Ibid.

[19] Ibid.

[20] This is an unedited transcript of most of Adam Dorn's letter to Ben's father. The complete letter was reprinted in *The Descendants of Peter and Sophia (Lauer) Ruth* by Jack Akerboom and Anna Ruth Salzman (Elverson, Pennsylvania: Mennonite Family History, 1994, page 491). The authors acquired it from the Civil War records of Benneville P. Ruth at the National Archives in Washington, D.C.

[21] Geoffrey C. Ward, with Ric Burns and Ken Burns, *The Civil War*.

[22] *Fold3*, Benneville P. Ruth (https://www.fold3.com/memorial/656053647/benneville-p-ruth-civil-war-stories: accessed June 20, 2023), database and images, https://www.fold3.com/memorial/656053647/benneville-p-ruth-civil-war-stories.

[23] Steve Smith, *Finding Benjamin Franklin Morse*.

[24] Geoffrey C. Ward, with Ric Burns and Ken Burns, *The Civil War*.

[25] There is a discrepancy regarding when Ben started his military service. Official military records show his enlistment date as January 1, 1864, with a muster date of February 16, 1864. However, both his field diary and a February 6, 1864, letter to his father indicate his service began as early as October of 1863.

[26] Steve Smith, *Finding Benjamin Franklin Morse*.

[27] Leander Stillwell, *The Story of a Common Soldier of Army Life in the Civil War, 1861-1865* (Kansas City: Franklin Hudson Publishing Company, 1920), 104–05.

[28] Geoffrey C. Ward, with Ric Burns and Ken Burns, *The Civil War*.

[29] Sam R. Watkins, *Co. Aytch* (Nashville, Tennessee: Cumberland Presbyterian Publishing House, 1882) 142, 143.

[30] Steve Smith, *Finding Benjamin Franklin Morse*.

[31] Ibid.

[32] Geoffrey C. Ward, with Ric Burns and Ken Burns, *The Civil War*.

CHAPTER SEVEN
Westward Ho: To the Heartland

[1] Anonymous, *The Northumberland County Historical Society, Proceedings and Addresses, Vol. 8* (Sunbury, Pennsylvania: Northumberland County Historical Society, 1936), 133, 135, 138, 154.

[2] Ibid.

[3] Ibid.

4 Anonymous, "Handout Materials," *Ruth Reunion – 250th Anniversary of Peter Ruth Coming to America*, (September 17-19, 1983), Materials distributed to attendees include itinerary, description of various Ruth properties, maps, land surveys, land grant indentures, estate settlement petition and miscellaneous other documents. Copies are in the possession of the author, Thomas Gerhart, president of the Pennsylvania German Society, and other family attendees.

5 *Wikipedia*, 2023, "Sunbury, Pennsylvania," Wikimedia Foundation, last modified April 28, 2023, 03:13, https://en.wikipedia.org/wiki/Sunbury%2C_Pennsylvania.

6 Anonymous, *Ruth Reunion – 250th Anniversary*.

7 Anonymous, *The Northumberland County Historical Society*.

8 Ruth Family Association of Illinois – 1st Annual Reunion, August 29, 1936, Chicago, Illinois, an address John Lowry Ruth gave to the association from printed materials distributed at the meeting. A copy of his presentation is in the author, Jim Ruth's, possession and can be found on Ancestry.com under Ruth–Null Family Tree, in the account of Kathy Ruth under Johann Peter Ruth and/or his descendants in the Gallery section.

9 George Rogers Taylor, *Transportation Revolution* (New York: Holt, Reinhart and Winston, 1964), 79.

10 Anonymous, "The National Road," *National Park Service*, last updated June 12, 2022, https://www.nps.gov/articles/national-road.htm.

11 Anonymous, "The National Road US 40 Washington Street," *This Is Indiana*, accessed April 29, 2023, https://thisisindiana.angelfire.com/nationalroadi40washington.htm.

12 Kathy Alexander, "The National Road – First Highway in America," *Legends of America*, last updated April 2022, https://www.legendsofamerica.com/ah-nationalroad/.

13 Anonymous, "The National Road," *National Park Service*.

14 Anonymous, "The National Road US 40 Washington Street."

15 Anonymous, *Portrait and Biographical Album of Stephenson County, Illinois* (Chicago: Chapman Brothers, 1888), 543.

16 Ibid.

17 Anonymous, *The History of Stephenson County, Illinois* (Chicago: Western Historical Company, 1880), 182.

18 Ibid.

19 US Congress, *US Statutes at Large*, Volume 3, 13th through 18th Congress (United States), 566. https://www.loc.gov/item/llsl-v3/

20 *Wikipedia*, 2023, "Land Act of 1820," Wikimedia Foundation, last modified February 5, 2023, 16:52, https://en.wikipedia.org/wiki/Land_Act_of_1820.

21 *U. S. General Land Office Records*, U. S. Department of the Interior, Bureau of Land Management, March 10, 1843, accessed May 2, 2023, https://glorecords.blm.gov/details/patent/default.aspxaccession=IL0860__.154&docClass=STA&sid=25sbr3mg.g31#patentDetailsTabIndex=1.

22 Virginia L. Park, *Long Grove Lore and Legend.* Long Grove Historical Society, 1978, 7.

23 Bureau of Land Management, U. S. General Land Office Records for George Ruth, dated 3/10/1843, Lake County, IL, Document #7811, BLM serial number IL NO S/N.

24 *Ruth Family Association of Illinois – 4th Annual Reunion*, August 26, 1939, Lake Zurich, Illinois, Chester (Chet) Ruth presiding, from minutes of the meeting distributed to attendees. A copy of his presentation is in the author's possession, Jim Ruth, and can be found on Ancestry.com under the Ruth-Null Family Tree, an account of Kathy Ruth, under Johann Peter Ruth and/or his descendants in the Gallery section.

25 Anonymous, *Ruth Reunion – 250th Anniversary.*

26 *Find a Grave*, memorial page for George W Washburn (4 Jul 1847–13 May 1862), Memorial ID 215456006, maintained by Dennis Skalstad (contributor 50144687), accessed April 30, 2023, https://www.findagrave.com/memorial/215456006/george-w-washburn.

27 *Ruth Family Association of Illinois – 4th Annual Reunion.*

28 Esther Ruth Smith, *Genealogical History Chart - William Ruth.* (Family genealogist and historian, Esther Ruth Smith collected a voluminous number of documents—genealogical charts, letters, newspaper clippings, etc.—regarding the Ruth/Smith families, and their trees. In 2022, Steve Smith, the curator of Esther's records, took more than 1,500 individual photos of the family's historical memorabilia in her files. He emailed copies to me and other extended family members. One of those items photographed, a family genealogical chart on William Ruth, included notes referencing William's move west in 1836.)

29 Anonymous, *Portrait and Biographical Album of Stephenson County, Illinois* (Chicago: Chapman Brothers, 1888), 543.

30 Ibid.

31 Ibid.

32 Anonymous, *Ruth Reunion – 250th Anniversary.*

33 Anonymous, "Obituary of Deacon William Ruth," *The Mantorville Express*, October 16, 1903, 1.

34 Anonymous, "The Tickets – Prohibition," *The Mantorville Express*, October 31, 1890, 3.

35 Anonymous, *History of Winona, Olmsted, and Dodge Counties* (Chicago: H. H. Hill and Company,1884), 858, 862, 866, 867, 871, 872, 874, 875.

36 Ibid.

37 Anonymous, "Obituary of Deacon William Ruth."

38 Anonymous, "Mrs. S. Ruth Passes Away At Anderson Home," *The Daily People's Press*, February 15, 1920, unnumbered inside page.

39 *Wikipedia*, 2023. "Mazeppa, Minnesota," Wikimedia Foundation, last modified February 17, 2023, 21:40, https://en.wikipedia.org/wiki/Mazeppa%2C_Minnesota.

40 Anonymous, "Last Rites Held For Minnie Ruth Friday," *The Mantorville Express*, October 17, 1935, 1.

41 Anonymous, "The Beginnings of Mazeppa," *Mazeppa Area Historical Society*, accessed April 29, 2023, www.mazeppahistoricalsociety.org/the-beginning-of-Mazeppa.html.

42 Anonymous, *Mazeppa Tribune* (Mazeppa, MN), May 16, 1888.

43 Anonymous, *Ruth Reunion – 250th Anniversary*.

44 Ibid.

45 Ibid.

46 Ibid.

47 Anonymous, "Last Rites Held For Minnie Ruth Friday."

48 Anonymous, "C. Walker Passes Away," *The Schaller Herald*, November 2, 1933.

CHAPTER EIGHT

The World Wars: More Sacrifices on the Altar of Freedom

1 Anonymous, "Shadows of War," *Library of Congress*, accessed June 3, 2023, 16:06, https://www.loc.gov/classroom-materials/immigration/german/shadows-of-war/.

2 Anonymous, "Sergeant Ruth Passes On," *Unknown Newspaper*, around September 1918, (Loose article clipped from a newspaper; the paper's name is missing, found among the archives of Ruth family historian Esther Ruth Smith).

3 Ibid.

4 American Battle Monuments Commission, *American Armies and Battlefields in Europe* (Washington, DC: United States Government Printing Office, 1938), 408, 410, 411.

5 Anonymous, "Sergeant Ruth Passes On."

6 Ibid.

7 Anonymous, "Ruth Fell Leading Charge," *Unknown Newspaper*, around 1919, (Loose article clipped from a newspaper; the paper's name is missing, found among the archives of Ruth family historian Esther Ruth Smith).

8 Anonymous, "Sergeant Ruth Passes On."

[9] Salvatore Mercogliano, "We Built Her to Bring Them Over There," *Sea History,* no. 161 (Winter 2017-2018): 18–20.

[10] Ibid.

[11] Ibid.

[12] Raymond A. Mann and amended by Christopher B. Havern Sr., "Von Steuben I (Id. No. 3017)," *Naval History and Heritage Command,* published May 8, 2018, 07:18:43 EDT https://www.history.navy.mil/research/histories/ship-histories/danfs/v/von-steuben-i.html.

[13] Anonymous, "Agamemnon," *History Central,* accessed May 28, 2023, 10:08, https://www.historycentral.com/navy/Steamer/Agamemnon.html.

[14] Anonymous, "World War I Battlefield Companion," *American Battle Monuments Commission*, July 2018, 6, 36, 117, 118.

[15] Ibid.

[16] Ibid.

[17] Vin Mannix, "Wonderful Wanderlust," *Boca Raton News*, February 24, 1997, 3A.

CHAPTER NINE
Arlington: The Beautiful City of the Dead

[1] Congressional Record, *Proceedings and Debates of the Second Session of the Seventy-Fourth Congress of the United States of America* (Washington: United States Government Printing Office, 1936), 1153.

[2] Anonymous, "About New Commandant, Matron, Soldiers Home" *The Sandusky Register*, October 5, 1921, 1.

[3] Anonymous, "Perry L. Null Dead; Burial In Washington, D.C." *The Sandusky Register Star-News*, September 27, 1941, 1.

[4] Charles B. Galbreath, *History of Ohio* (New York and Chicago: The American Historical Society, Inc., 1925), 329.

[5] H. L. Peeke, *The Centennial History of Erie County, Ohio* (United States: Penton Press Company, 1925), 233, 236–37.

[6] Terrance P. McHugh, *With the Help of Strangers* (Chapin, South Carolina: Self-Published, 2021), 20, 25, 26, 73, 83, 84, 89.

[7] Ibid.

[8] Ibid.

[9] Ibid.

10 Robert W. Ruth, *The Ruths, Vol. I–V,* In the 1990s, Robert Ruth assembled a set of five family history albums from boxes of old letters, photographs, and other family memorabilia. Every page is filled with family photographs, each with identifying captions or a short narrative description of family life and the times in which they lived. Some pages contain colorfully illustrated maps he drew, while others have photocopies of newspaper front pages highlighting momentous world events.

11 Ibid.

12 Ibid.

13 Ibid.

14 Ibid.

About the Author

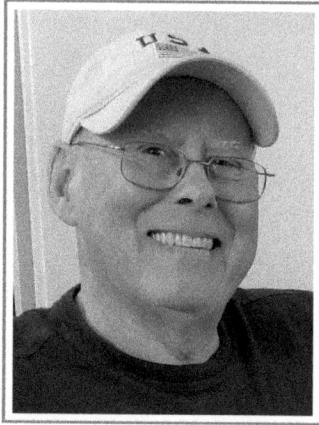

JIM RUTH is a graduate of the University of Maryland with a double major in business and journalism. Although his profession took him into the business world as a Certified Financial Planner, he found time over his forty-year career to follow his passion for writing, with over three hundred published articles to his credit. His expansive writings have appeared in numerous local and national periodicals—from an article on childhood learning disabilities in *ADDitude* magazine to editorials in the *Washington Post* and the *Chicago Tribune*. His award-winning monthly column, Managing Money, appeared for five years in two national magazines (*Advisor Today* and *Retirement Life*) up until his retirement.

An American history buff, Jim developed a keen interest in genealogy after discovering his ancestors came to America in 1733. *The Pursuit* is his first book endeavor.

www.thepursuit4u.com
email: jim@thepursuit4u.com

Milton Keynes UK
Ingram Content Group UK Ltd.
UKHW040212210924
448601UK00012B/210/J